PIERRE CORAN

Fables à l'air du temps

Fables in a Modern Key

English Translations by Norman R. Shapiro

Illustrations by Olga Pastuchiv

PIERRE CORAN

Fables à l'air du temps

Fables in a
Modern Key

English Translations by Norman R. Shapiro

Illustrations by Olga Pastuchiv

Black Widow Press wishes to thank Wesleyan University for its support. Publication of this book has been aided by a grant from the Thomas and Catharine McMahon Fund of Wesleyan University, established through the generosity of the late Joseph McMahon.

Black Widow Press is an imprint of Commonwealth Books, Inc., Boston, MA. Distributed to the trade by NBN (National Book Network) throughout North America, Canada, and the U.K. All Black Widow Press books are printed on acid-free paper, and glued into bindings. Black Widow Press and its logo are registered trademarks of Commonwealth Books, Inc.

Joseph S. Phillips and Susan J. Wood, Ph.D., Publishers
www.blackwidowpress.com

Illustrations and Art Direction: Olga Pastuchiv
Design, Typesetting & Production: Kerrie Kemperman

ISBN-13: 978-0-9960079-1-7

Printed in the United States

10 9 8 7 6 5 4 3 2 1

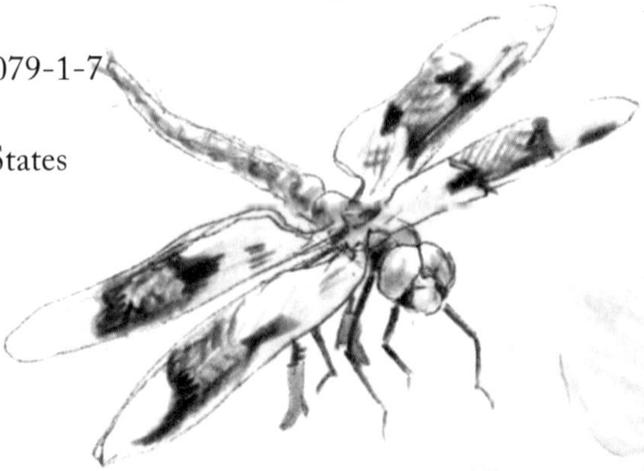

Où est l'impossible
puisqu'une chenille finit, tôt ou tard,
par voler ?

Where is the impossible
since a caterpillar, sooner or later,
eventually goes flying?

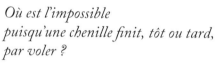

*This collection is dedicated with gratitude
to the long and happy memory of two dear friends
who most certainly would have enjoyed it,
Caldwell and Camilla Titcomb*

CONTENTS

A mon ami Norman,

LA LIBELLULE ET LE POETE

Dans la maison d'un poète,
Une libellule entra.
Elle vole, çà et là
Mais une vitre l'arrête.
Le poète l'aperçoit.
Il la rassure à mi-voix
Puis lui rend la liberté.
Dehors, à l'heure du thé,
La demoiselle revient
Et se pose sur la main,
Sur l'épaule du poète
Surpris et quelque peu fier
De revoir la prisonnière
Qui paraît lui faire fête.
Le fin fond de cette histoire
Reste encore à deviner.
Est-ce un merci, un hasard
Ou des ondes échangées ?

La morale y est cachée.
A chacun de l'énoncer !

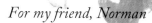

For my friend, Norman

THE DRAGONFLY AND THE POET

Into a poet's house there flew
A dragonfly, darting about
A window that could let her out.
But it stood shut. What could she do,
Save stop, entrapped, imprisoned there?
The poet, with the tenderest air,
Gave her her freedom, graciously…
That afternoon, at garden-tea,
Back flew the same winged damsel, and
Gently lit on the poet's hand,
Then on his shoulder, lightly set.
Surprised and rather proud was he
To see her pay her freedom's debt
With joyous reciprocity!…
Yes, there's a meaning here. But best
That it, rather than told, be guessed:
A favor?… Grace?… The merest chance?…
A shared poetic resonance?

The hidden moral? Who can say?
It's yours to find it where you may.

TRANSLATOR'S PREFACE

Throughout his long career, Pierre Coran (*pseudo.* Eugène Delaisse) has distinguished himself as one of Belgium's pre-eminent French-language writers of children's literature. It is not by accident that he has an elementary school named for him in his native city of Mons. As a poet, he has adopted the fable genre as his own, tuning his special brand of whimsy to the lyre of his model, the immortal Jean de La Fontaine, modulated into a modern key.

But, like his models, Coran's fables—especially those of the present collection—are really children's fare in tradition only. Though La Fontaine's early fables were, in fact, penned for the edification of the young, as his career progressed they grew more and more profoundly philosophical, eventually surpassing young people's appreciation in both their sophistication of subject and, no less, their elegance of style. Readers will find, I think, that Coran is likewise a "children's poet" in name only. They will see him taking pleasure in adapting his preferred genre to scenarios of a subtlety beyond the ken of the average child, and capriciously replete with 21st-century technology and social concerns, treated with a wry deftness that few youngsters would be expected to grasp. Indeed, if Coran the stylist can be said to write for children, it is "for the child in all of us", as he himself has said. Punster *extraordinaire,* he clearly delights in coining words when the occasion demands—and even when it doesn't! One thinks of the

wordplay of a Prévert or a Queneau. His collection *Jaffabules* is a typical example, creating for its title a noun that is, at the same time, a homophone of the verb *j'affabule,* "I tell tales"—a declaration attested to by his several novels and his more than 130 stories. For children…? Well…

Born in 1934 and currently living with his wife in the village of Jurbise, in the Walloon province of Hainaut, this mercurial man of letters has followed several simultaneous careers. As an educator, he has taught at both ends of the academic scale, elementary and advanced, the latter as professor of literary history at the Conservatoire Royal de Mons. At the same time he has indulged his creative talents as novelist, screenplay author, prolific writer of animated cartoon soundtracks, and, especially, poet. His honors are many, among them the Prix Jean de La Fontaine, in 1976, and the first Grand Prix de Poésie pour la Jeunesse, in 1989. Likewise his works, of which *Fables à l'air du temps* (2013) is one of his most recent. When he sent me the unpublished manuscript several months ago, I found these modern fables in antique dress irresistible and thought that I might translate a few to surprise him. But the surprise was soon mine, as those "few," week by week, became the present complete collection.

I am happy to count Pierre Coran among my friends, and I offer his work to an English-speaking readership with the greatest of pleasure.

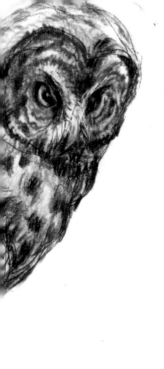

LE HIBOU ET LES VANITEUX

Au zoo d'Anvers, trois pensionnaires
Se vantaient d'avoir accompli
      Par défi
Des exploits extraordinaires.
Un des hiboux s'approcha d'eux
Et demanda aux vaniteux :
« Qui a creusé les mers et mis de l'eau dedans ?
— C'est moi ! dit l'éléphant.
— Et qui a découvert les volcans, les déserts ?
— Moi ! dit le dromadaire.
— Qui allume la lune, les étoiles, le soir ?
— C'est moi ! dit l'aigle noir. »
Un orage subit s'abattit sur le zoo
    Avec vent et vacarme.
    Du bec, les deux oiseaux
    Actionnèrent l'alarme.
    Une hutte puis deux
    Tout à coup prirent feu.
La pluie aidant, le dromadaire
Et l'éléphant les arrosèrent.
    Lors le zoo en danger
    Et en plein désarroi,
    Grâce à tous, fut sauvé.
    « Au lieu des moi, moi, moi,
    Dire nous, c'est bien mieux,
    Hulula le hibou,
    Tout seuls, nous pouvons peu
    Mais ensemble beaucoup. »

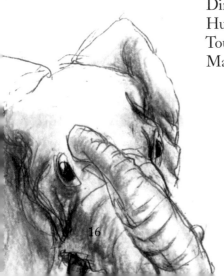

THE OWL AND THE BRAGGARTS

Three Antwerp Zoo inhabitants
Were boasting, each of circumstance
Extraordinaire, in which the three,
            Challenged—defied
By a most dire emergency—
With exploit most adroit replied…
An owl approached the braggarts. "Who
Was it, my friends… Which one of you
Hollowed the land and filled it with the sea?"
            The elephant blares: "Me!"
"And, pray tell, who was it that first
Braved the volcanoes and the deserts' thirst?"
"Me!" squeals the dromedary. "And
Which of you makes the moon and stars grow bright?"
"Me!" shrieks the eagle, black as night…
Just then, a storm is loosed upon the land.
            Winds a-howl rage over the zoo…
            Rain fire… First one, then two
            Enclosures flame, a-flare…
            Eagle and Owl—deft pair—
            Pull with their beaks and sound
The fire alarm… And, from the rain-soaked ground,
Elephant sprays and dromedary spits
            The zoo to safety! * "Thanks to its
            'Us' rather than its 'me, me, me,'
            The zoo is saved. Whence one can see,"
            Hoots Owl, "useless is only one.
When 'one' turns 'many', much, indeed is done."

---

* The reference is to the well-known nasty habit of camels, dromedaries,
  llamas, vicuñas, and the like to spit at the slightest provocation.

17

LES DEUX CHATONS

Un joli chaton de maison
Rencontra au creux d'un sentier
Un long chaton de noisetier.
En forêt, il est de bon ton
D'engager la conversation.
Ce que s'empressent donc de faire
Les deux chatons peu ordinaires.
Le premier avoue qu'il regrette
D'être un chat, non une noisette
Pour vivre caché sous les feuilles
A la barbe des écureuils.
Le second aurait tant voulu
Etre un beau matou moustachu
Comme on en voit ramper, le soir,
Les yeux flamboyant dans le noir.
Quand, à regret, ils se quittèrent,
Un des ramiers de la clairière,
Les entendant, leur roucoula :
« Les matous sont comme les hommes,
Les noisettes comme les chats.
Les uns rêvent qu'ils sont en somme
Ce que d'autres ne veulent pas. »

THE TWO KITTENS

Two kittens met… One, usually
An indoor cat, a stay-at-home,
And one who called a hazel tree
Her dwelling… Now, when creatures roam
The forest paths, as did these two
That day—rare for the first, at that,
Who seldom quit his habitat—
It's only proper that they do
The courteous thing: stop, have a chat…
And so they did. Our household cat
Said that he wished that he might be
A hazelnut, and make the tree
His home, leaf-hidden… Sneer, and tell
Squirrels: "Go hide your nuts in hell!"
At which, the second said that he
Would be a puss, mustachioed,
Like those one sees in Man's abode,
Eyes flashing in the night!… When they,
Sad to leave, turn and go their way,
An owl who, in the clearing, had
Listened to what each had to say,
Hooted a cooing sigh: "Egad!
Tomcats, and men, and hazelnuts!
They're all the same! No ifs, no buts…
Every one has his dreams, and, yearns
To be the one the other spurns!"

LE LOUP ET LA TORTUE

Un loup gourmand a confondu
Un sandwich et une tortue.

AÏE ! AÏE ! AÏE !

D'un seul coup, sur la carapace,
Les dents du loup gourmand se cassent.

AÏE ! AÏE ! AÏE !

Depuis lors, l'édenté flapi
Avale, sans grand appétit,
Soupe, rata, bouillon, bouillie
Compote, jus et petits pots
De marmelade d'abricots
Et confiture de myrtilles.
En repartant tête dehors,
La tortue crie au carnivore :

« Tout gourmand, tard ou tôt,
Est puni de son défaut. »

THE WOLF AND THE TURTLE

Turtle or sandwich? Sense askew,
Gluttonous wolf confused the two.

Ay Ay! Ay Ay! Ay Ay!

One bite and, all at once—alack!—
Gluttonous wolf's teeth crumble, crack!

Ay Ay! Ay Ay! Ay Ay!

Whereat the toothless popinjay—
Appetite gone—now eats but little:
No victual solid, stout, or brittle…
Flans, jams, and juices, fruit *sorbets*,
Soups, ratatouille, all mush and mash,
Jellies, and hash, and succotash…
Leaving, the turtle—head poked out—
Gives the ex-carnivore a shout:

"Glutton, in time—yea, verily!—
Pays the price for his gluttony."

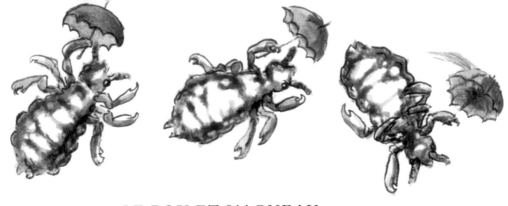

LE POU ET L'AGNEAU

Un pou prit congé d'un berger
Et s'installa sur un agneau
Qui dormait dans la bergerie.
Comme le poil était extra
Et qu'il s'y trouvait bien au chaud,
Il invita de la famille.
Le pou resta discret quand l'agneau s'éveilla
Et courut dans le pré rejoindre le troupeau.
Un chien le surveillait, que le pou trouva beau,
    Si beau qu'il décida
    D'abandonner l'agneau.
    Mais quand le gardien, las
    De courir la prairie,
    Plongea dans la rivière,
Le pou se retrouva collé à une pierre
Au bord d'un champ de blé et loin de sa famille.
De nos jours, l'inconstant occupe le chapeau
D'un mannequin géant qui effraie les oiseaux.

    Qui change de monture
    Au gré de ses élans,
    Sans zèle ou démesure
    Se doit d'être prudent.

THE LOUSE AND THE LAMB

A certain louse there was, who had
Been living on a shepherd lad,
And who now took his leave, and chose
A tender lamb on whom to dwell,
Who, in the sheepfold lay a-doze…
So warm the pen, so beautiful
And bountiful his new host's wool,
That the mite thought he ought do well
To go tell all his kin and kith!
So, when the lamb awakes, he goes
Off to invite the flock… Forthwith,
Spying a hound, he finds he is
Finer still, and would make him his
New home… Whereat, our louse forsook
His present lamb-abode, and took
Up residence… But soon the hound,
Having his fill of bounding round
The pasture, dove into the brook,
And left the louse… Stock-still… Stuck to a stone,
Mid stalks of grain… Flock-less, alone!…
His home today? A scarecrow's hat!

The message in all that?
Would you attain your dream?
Contentment be your wont.
Sit pat! Be wise, and don't
Change horses in midstream.

LA MOUETTE ET LA BOUTEILLE

Un matin, sur une plage,
Entre crabes, coquillages,
Une mouette repère
Une bouteille à la mer.
Encre bleue sur papier blanc,
Un message y est dedans.
Du bec, l'oiseau le retire
Mais puisqu'il ne sait pas lire,
Il propose le papier
Au commandant d'un navire
Aussi curieux qu'étonné.
Comme à une confidente,
Le marin lit le message
A la mouette impatiente :
« Si tu rêves de voyage
Sachant que tu ne pars pas,
A l'image des nuages,
Tu peux voyager en toi. »
C'est ce que fit la mouette
Juchée sur la girouette
D'un immeuble avoisinant.
Elle vit voler, en elle,
Un nuage d'hirondelles
Bec et ailes dans le vent.

THE SEAGULL AND THE BOTTLE

Midst many a crab and shell
Strewn on the shore, pell-mell,
A bottle that had been—
Doubtless—cast in the sea,
Lies there, invitingly.
A seagull peers within,
Spies a note—paper white,
Ink blue—and, with her bill,
Pokes, prods, and pulls, until
She works it free. But, quite
Frustrated, she cannot—
Unlettered bird—read what
The paper says. Wherefore,
She finds a commodore—
Surprised, intrigued—and who
Reads her the message. Lo!
Anxious, she hears: *"If you,*
Stranger, dream you would go
Voyaging off, but know
There is no chance you will,
Do as the clouds. You still
Can fly, wind-swept, and find
Your voyage in the mind…"
And so she will, as she—
Weathercock-perching, high
Aloft—dreams that she follows
A wafting cloud of swallows,
Soft-blown, borne airily,
Wings, beaks against the sky…

LA TAUPE ET LA VACHE

Une taupe de la prairie
Quitta la nuit des galeries.
Elle acheta sur Internet
Un GPS et des lunettes
Puis au marché se paya cash
Une monumentale vache,
Une ombrelle en soie naturelle,
Un chapeau et des bottillons.
La campagne fleurait si bon
Et lui parut partout si belle
Que la myope, sous l'ombrelle,
Se réjouit à sa façon
De ne plus vivre terre à terre
Et d'avoir pris la décision
De bourlinguer dans la lumière.
Dès son arrivée à la ville
Où l'air ambiant ne sent pas bon,
La taupe changea d'opinion.
Sa vache dut faire la file
Parmi les autos, les camions
Sous les quolibets de piétons
Que pareille bête horripile.
La taupe alors fit demi-tour,
Suivit la voix de la sagesse
Et celle de son GPS
Puis au terme de ce séjour,
Offrit l'ombrelle payée cash
Et ses lunettes à sa vache
Qui lui rumina, comme il sied,
Le mufle chaud et sans rancœur :

« Si le bonheur est dans le pré,
A quoi bon le chercher ailleurs. »

THE MOLE AND THE COW

A meadow mole there was, who thought
It meet, one night, to leave her lair.
Surfing the Internet, she bought
Herself a GPS, a pair
Of spectacles, a monstrous cow—
For cash!—a real silk parasol,
A hat, fine booties too… And now,
Off she goes with her wherewithal…
Ah! How fragrant the country round,
How fair to her myopic eyes!
Thought she: "How sweet, how worldly-wise
Was I to quit my underground
Abode, ramble beneath the skies
Bathed all in light!" But when she comes
To town, no more encomiums
To her surroundings! Foul, the air…
Clumsy, the cow, a-straggle there,
Struggling against auto and truck,
As passers-by jape, jibe—dumbstruck—
Staring at beast the likes of her!
At length, our hole-bred *voyageur*,
Yielding to reason's worldliness
(And to her trusty GPS),
Turned tail—chastened adventurer
Undone!—gave Cow specs, parasol,
And all her cash-paid folderol.
Cow, in a mood gently to chide her,
Mooed her a moral to deride her:

"Meadow-ground suits Mole? Well, pray let her
Not wander round in search of better!"

LE PIVERT ET LE SONGE

Un soir, les oiseaux du monde
S'arrêtèrent de chanter,
C'est du moins ce que raconte
Un pivert de la vallée
Aux moineaux qui vagabondent
Nuit et jour, de haie en haie.
Ce soir-là, sans nulle honte,
La lune s'est recouchée,
Elle rangea ses marées
Et en oublia la Terre.
Le Soleil eut moins envie
D'éclairer un univers
Où le chant n'est plus que bruit.
Alors, contraint et forcé,
L'humain cessa désormais
De détruire les forêts
Où la faune surabonde
Et tous les oiseaux du monde
Se remirent à chanter
Dès la rosée du matin.
C'est toujours ce que soutient
Le pivert de la vallée,
Aussi bavard qu'indiscret,
Sans que son bec ne s'allonge.

Si cette fable est un mensonge,
Elle a sa part de vérité.

THE JACKDAW AND THE DREAM

In every land, birds—one twilight—
Stopped singing! (Or, so it was said
By a green jackdaw, valley-bred,
To swallows in their skimming flight
From hedge to hedge, all day, all night).
The Moon went toddling off to bed,
Tucked up her tides, forgot the Earth...
The Sun thought it was scarcely worth
His time to light a universe
Where song is merely noise—or worse!
Therewith, the human population
Was forced to cease deforestation
Of fauna's wildlife dwellings. And,
Again, the birds in every land
And nation now began to sing
Their morning-song, tweet-twittering
Once more as daylight, glittering, spanned
The dew... (At least, so it was said
By a green jackdaw, valley-bred:
A babbler? True. And yet, his beak
Didn't grow longer, so to speak.) *

This tale? A lie! But, understand,
It tells the truth. More than a shred!

---

*   The reference, internationally recognizable, is to
    Pinocchio, whose nose grew with each lie he told.

LA MYGALE ET LA FOURMI

Dans le repaire terre et toile
D'une monstrueuse mygale,
Un jour, s'empêtre une fourmi
Qui ne retrouve plus son nid,
Fourmi ailée de belle taille
Et d'une fragile beauté
Se débattant, vaille que vaille,
Pour recouvrer la liberté.
« Libérez-moi ! Je vous en prie !
Faites preuve de courtoisie.
Moi, la fourmi, vous, la mygale,
Nous ne sommes pas des rivales.
On vous écrase, on m'empoisonne.
Qui nous aime vraiment ? Personne ! »
L'araignée dont les yeux s'avivent
Se rapproche de la captive :
« Vous avouerai-je, sans façon,
Que je nourris quelque appétit,
Pour un lézard, une souris,
Un frelon, une libellule
Voire une proie plus minuscule
Que je me sers à l'occasion. »
La fourmi s'inquiète, à raison,
De cet aveu et balbutie :
« Vous me voyez comme je suis :
Maigre à en être ridicule
Et ne pourrais en aucun cas

THE HAIRY SPIDER AND THE ANT

A hairy spider, looking much
Like a tarantula or such,
One day, trapped in her lair, an ant—
The wingèd kind—of elegant
Proportions… Fragile beauty, she
Flails, whips about, poor supplicant,
Begging for her lost liberty.
"Free me, I pray! No rivals, you
And I…! Alas! It's all too true!
Man steps on you and poisons me!
Nobody loves us…" Hearing which,
Spider, eyes leering, quits her niche
And slithers toward her prisoner-prize.
"Would you believe, despite my size,"
Says she, "I have an appetite
For lizards, mice, wasps, dragon-flies…
And smaller prey as well, who might
Find, on occasion, that they share
The honors of my bill of fare!"
The ant grows anxious—and for cause!—
Stammering: "Look… I… Look at me…
I… You can see…" She hems and haws…
"This is all that I am! You see
All that there is… Absurdly small!
Why, I'm nothing to eat at all!"
"Who knows? Who knows?" derides the spider,
Licking her chops, and squats beside her…

Etre au menu de vos repas.
— Qui sait ? Qui sait ? dit la mygale
En s'aiguisant les mandibules.
Un rien apaise une fringale. »
C'est alors qu'une jardinière
Pour le moins inhospitalière,
Armée comme un gladiateur
Le terrier tape avec vigueur.
     Mais, maladroite,
      Elle dérape et rate
Notre fourmi qui met les voiles
      A dos de mygale.

Péril commun :
          Deux ne font qu'un.

Suddenly, gladiatrix-like, *
Harridan, armed with pole and spike—
Garden tools—pokes at Spider's hole…
She trips… She slips… Misses her goal,
       As fall askew
         Her spike and pole…
Set free, out crawls our harried Spider,
On her back, Ant, a wing-spread rider…

When danger lurks under the sun,
       What works for two?
       Let two be one!

---

*   I'm rather certain that there were no female gladiators in Roman times, but know that, had there been, this feminine form would have been used. (I take this opportunity to strike a blow for the reinstatement of a useful suffix that has fallen victim to the abuse of linguistic equality.)

LE ZOO BIZARRE ET LA CHORALE

Le zoo de Zanzibar,
Est un jardin bizarre.
  Deux hulottes
Y tricotent
  Des pulls
Pour un pitbull,
Un des zébus zélé
Shampouine un chimpanzé.
Deux gnous font du judo.
Un loup joue du piano
Et un zèbre au yo-yo
Avec un escargot.
Aussi zen qu'un Bouddha,
Un yack fait du yoga.
Mais dès que la chorale
Des loris, des aras
Et autres volatiles,
A l'heure des repas,
Commence un récital,
Si mélodieux soit-il,
Le zoo devient désert
Comme un parc en hiver.

« Ventre affamé n'a pas d'oreilles :
C'est connu ! » craille une corneille.

THE BIZARRE ZOO AND THE CHORALE

Bizarre, bizarre, that zoo
In Zanzibar, where two
Lady owls sit and knit
    Sweaters to fit
    A pet pitbull…
Where one of the zebus—
Resolutely and full
Of energy—shampoos
A chimp… Where, too, two gnus
Do judo moves… And where
A wolf, devil-may-care,
Tickles the piano-keys
As he accompanies
A zebra, spinning there
A snail, flipped through the air
In yo-yo wise—out, back,
Up down… And where a yak
Follows the paths of Zen,
Yogi adept… But when,
Come mealtimes, and the bird
Chorale—parrots, macaws,
And all—would fain be heard
Singing to the applause
Of visitors, the latter,
Stomachs a-growl, turn, scatter.
Desert the zoo, now grown
Like park in winter snow: alone!

"A hungry belly has no ears!"
    So caws a crow.
    Alas, quite so…
(The proverb has been known for years.)

L'HIPPOPOTAME ET LE CHEVAL

Le hasard parfois porte chance
A qui pèche par ignorance.

Dans un parc d'attractions, un jeune hippopotame
      Rêvait d'être un cheval
      Que le public acclame,
Un cheval d'hippodrome ou de garde royale.
Dès qu'il fermait les yeux, il trottait, sautillait,
      Paradait, galopait
      Avec ou sans jockey.
Son rêve l'empêchait de dépérir d'ennui
A la vue des curieux qui se méfiaient de lui.
Jusqu'au jour où survient un des guides du parc.
Le voyant, il claironne aux rameurs d'une barque :
« Avant de nous quitter, une dernière épreuve.
Ce jeune hippopotame a un surnom. Lequel ?
— Je sais, je sais, je sais ! crie une demoiselle.
En Afrique, un hippo est un cheval de fleuve. »
En apprenant cela, le bovidé en joie
      Que les bravos émeuvent
      Saute à l'eau et s'ébat.
      Les rameurs font naufrage.

THE HIPPOPOTAMUS WHO WOULD BE A HORSE

When, ignorant, one has a whim,
Sometimes luck grants his wish to him.

A hippopotamus, young denizen
Of an amusement park, dreamt that he was
　　A horse—one doting on applause
　　Of devotees equestrian,
Hippodrome-bound; or, for another, who
Would proudly strut in regal retinue.
Whenever he would shut his eyes in sleep,
He would be coursing there—a-trot, a-leap,
　　　A-gallop—jockey-led
　　　Or even jockey-less.
Only his dream it was, I must confess,
That kept this would-be horse from dying, dead
Of boredom, as onlookers leered and eyed
Him with disdain... Until a tourist-guide
Spotted him on the "Jungle River" ride,
And cried: "Let's see how smart we are! Who knows
A nickname for that hippopotamus?"
"I do! I do!" a young miss—loud, brash—rose
To the occasion, and, vociferous,

Certains, tout aussitôt, se sauvent à la nage
Et d'autres au petit trot
A cheval sur l'hippo.

Une autre fin, je gage, eût été bien dommage.

Vowed that "in Africa the hippo goes
Under the name of 'river horse!'"* The beast,
    Most overjoyed, to say the least,
To many a bravo, splashes and cavorts,
    Sinking the boat... The ride aborts.
Some tourists swim, a-grumble and a-curse.
        The rest are forced—alas, alack—
        To waddle out on hippo-back.

Still, for all that, it might have ended worse.

---

* The precocious young classical scholar was, of course, referring to the
  etymology of the name, from the Greek compound *hippos potamou*,
  "horse of the river."

L'EPEIRE ET LE BABOUIN

Avec la plume d'un héron,
Un babouin peint des aquarelles.
C'est un artiste de renom
Dont l'aura est universelle,
Artiste en vue, artiste en vogue
Si l'on en croit son catalogue.
Le soir de l'inauguration
De sa nouvelle exposition,
Le public est au rendez-vous,
Tout en beauté, en élégance,
En discours et en convenances.
Un cri retentit tout à coup.
C'est qu'au plafond haut de la salle,
Une araignée tisse sa toile
Avec soin et habileté.

La responsable de l'expo,
Au comble de l'indignité,
Se démène et crie au complot,
Réclame une brosse et s'écrie:
« Il faut gommer cette infamie
En ce soir où l'Art est en fête
Autour d'un génie, d'un poète. »
S'ensuivent quelques trémolos.
A ce moment, l'aquarelliste
Intervient et clame au micro
A l'adresse de l'assemblée :

THE SPIDER AND THE BABOON

With heron-feather brush, an ape—
Baboon *aquarelliste* renowned,
Painter of many a fine landscape
And such—was hailed the wide world round,
Feted, admired… Among the very
Best of *artistes* extraordinary
(If one believes his catalogue)…
One night, his public customary
Attends an opening, all agog—
As usual, with much bla-bla-bla,
Chic as can be—when, suddenly,
A frantic shout blares out: "Oh!… Ah!…
Up there!… The ceiling!…" And they see
A spider swinging side to side,
Skillfully, calmly occupied
Spinning her web. The exposition's
Shocked impresario, most nonplussed,
Abashed at this worst of seditions,
Calls for a broom. Cries he: "We must
Sweep away that indignity!
On a night when we proudly fete
Genius and Art and Poetry,
It is not right that we should let…"
Et cetera… Whereat there rumbled
Tremolos of approval from
The chichi auditorium…

« Autant d'indignation m'attriste !
Qui voue du respect aux artistes
Se doit d'honorer l'araignée,
Une tisserande modèle.
Sa toile vaut mes aquarelles. »
Sur ce, chacun leva son verre
A la santé de cette épeire
Par le babouin promue vedette.
La foule est parfois girouette.

42

At that, our baboon—duly humbled—
Calls for a microphone. Says he:
"Such indignation troubles me.
You say we honor Art. If true,
Behold the spider! How can you
Deny that my mere *aquarelles*
Bear not the slightest parallel
To what she weaves! Scarce can I hold
A candle to her Art untold!…"
Moments before, quick to deride her,
The public—fickle weathervane—
Drinks toast on toast… Again, again…
In honor of the artist-spider!

LA GRUE ET LE PANDA

Mieux vaut, le plus souvent,
Qu'un conflit se termine
Ou se mette en sourdine
Avant qu'il soit navrant
Et qu'il ne s'enracine.
Ainsi qu'on va le voir
Au fil de cette histoire.

Sur la jonque de bois
D'un grand jardin chinois,
Une grue à cou blanc
Chantait, chantait sa joie
Aux poissons de l'étang.
Mais son chant dérangeait
Le panda d'à-côté
Qui lui hurla : « Assez !
Arrête donc de geindre.
Tu brises mes oreilles.
— Panda, vais-je me plaindre,
Lui répliqua l'oiseau,
Quand tu ronfles au soleil
Comme un chœur de crapauds ? »
A ces mots, tout à coup,
D'un rideau de bambous,
Une voix s'éleva,
Une voix magnifique.

THE CRANE AND THE PANDA

Lest they, at length, take root,
Best that our accusations
And our recriminations
End quickly, or grow mute.
Witness two beasts' dispute.

In China, in a park…
There, on a pond, a barque—
A simple junk of wood…
And on the junk there stood
A white-necked crane, whose song
Of joy, sung to the fish,
Annoyed, distressed the strong-
Willed panda—nasty-ish
Beast, I must say!—close by,
Who (right or wrong) will cry:
"Enough! Your chattering,
Whining, is shattering
My ears!" "Panda, do I
Complain," replies the crane,
"Or ask you to refrain
From snoring as you do—
Lolling out in the sun—
Like a toad-chorus who
Croaks, squawks, irks everyone?…"
Just then, there rises through

45

Alors, chacun se tut
Dans le jardin chinois,
Ecouta la musique,
Les coups de gong magiques
Et le vent à l'affût
Sur la jonque de bois.

A veil of frail bamboo,
Borne on the wind, a song
Magnificent. And they
Put their discord away,
Grow silent, listening to
The magic of a gong,
In China, in a park…
There, on a pond, a barque—
A simple junk of wood…

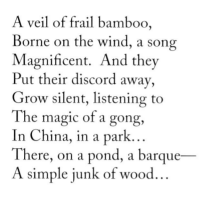

LE CHAT ET LE MIROIR

Un chat chic, chouchouté
Qui s'était refait le museau
Faisait de la publicité
Pour du rôti de dindonneau.
Quand il se vit à la télé,
Il proclama un peu partout :
« Je suis le plus beau des matous ! »
Mais à la foire du quartier,
    Le même soir,
    Dans un miroir,
Le vaniteux se trouva laid,
      Hideux,
      Affreux,
Plus tordu qu'un vilain serpent.
C'était un miroir déformant.

Qui vénère son image,
— Qu'il soit humain ou chat chic —
S'expose aux subtils mirages
De la chirurgie esthétique.

THE CAT AND THE MIRROR

A cat—a chic froufrou who'd had
A nose-job (a snout-job, that is)—
Big in the "advertising biz,"
Pitchman for a roast turkey ad
That showed all over the TV,
Saw his face shining on the screen.
"Never," he meowed—vowed—was there seen
Another physiognomy
Pretty as mine, I guarantee!"
          But, come that night,
          When, at the fair,
He looks into a mirror there,
He's faced with quite a frightening sight!
          Vain, debonair
No more! Now here's a how-de-do!
          Face all askew,
Vile, twisted serpent! Not a cat!…
One of those Fun House mirrors, that!

Whether chic cats or humans, we
Who worship, awed, our own reflections,
Might suffer the would-be corrections
     Of plastic surgery.

49

L'ARA ET LES CLIENTS

Au Grand Hôtel de Montpellier,
Un perroquet est exécré.
Les clients ne supportent plus
D'être éveillés par le chahut
Que le psittacidé prodigue.
Furieux, nombre d'entre eux se liguent,
Ils s'associent, ils pétitionnent
Pour qu'on le lie et le bâillonne.
Mais muet, l'ara ne peut l'être.
Le perroquet dit que son maître
Ne désire pas qu'il se taise :
Il est marchand de boules Quies.

Quand l'importun est opportun,
    Avec ou sans aide,
Bien malaisé est le remède.

50

THE MACAW AND THE GUESTS

In Montpellier—Le Grand Hôtel—
Lives a macaw, bird damned to hell
By sleepless guests! With "awk" and "quack" it
"Cawcaws" and squawks… Riled by the racket
Raised by said psittacitic beast,
The guests petition that, at least,
Someone should seize the parrot, tie it
Down, bound and gagged, and keep it quiet…
His parrot? Quiet? Certainly
Its owner never will agree.
Why? Selling earplugs is his trade!

When things that irk the *hoi polloi**
       Cause others joy,
There is no sure cure, I'm afraid.

---

*   I ask the reader's indulgence for this common but improper redundancy
   of the definite article in this English use of the Greek expression.

5

L'ABEILLE ET LE FRELON

Une abeille aimait un frelon
Et le frelon aimait l'abeille.
Tout s'annonçait sous le soleil
De la plus charmante façon.
Mise au parfum la reine mère
S'opposa à pareille union :
« Nos deux familles sont en guerre
Depuis des ans, des millénaires
Et, foi de moi, le resteront. »
Ce refus ne put que déplaire
Et à l'abeille et au frelon
Qui, d'un même élan, décidèrent
De fuir et changer d'horizon.
Si l'on en croit un papillon
Voltigeur devant l'éternel,
Il paraît vrai que tous deux vendent,
Des pollens, du miel de lavande
Sur le chemin de Compostelle,
Où jamais les reines ne vont.

Dans la vie, il est des tunnels
Qui créent de nouveaux horizons.

THE BEE AND THE WASP

A wasp there was who loved a bee,
Who loved the wasp reciprocally.
And the sun shone its charm upon
The pair of lovers… But, anon,
Would the queen mother—meddler, she!—.
Catch wind of their fair liaison.
"Impossible! Our family
And his," she cried, "have been at war
For centuries. Nay, even more!
And may they, 'sfaith! forever be!…"
The bee and wasp, stricken heart-sore
By this refusal, presently
Flee to a change of scenery…
According to a butterfly—
Winged comrade of eternity—
It seems a wealthy trade they ply
In pollen and lavender honey,
Living handsomely on the money
Of pilgrims Compostela-bound
(With never a queen bee to be found!).

Where tunnel-darkness cramps our eyes,
Often bright new horizons rise.

L'AÏ ET L'ETIQUETTE

Une nuit, à Paris, au grand Jardin des Plantes,
Un aï aperçut une étoile filante.
Comme il se doit en pareil cas, il fit un vœu :
Celui de ne plus être appelé paresseux.
Dès lors, il s'évertue à ôter l'étiquette
Dont il est affublé partout sur la planète.
Décidé, courageux, d'arbre en arbre, il excelle
Aux anneaux, au trapèze, aux barres parallèles.

            Efforts vains !

Aujourd'hui comme hier et sans doute demain,
L'aï est défini : édenté mammifère
Surnommé paresseux dans tous les dictionnaires.
        Le sachant, une belette
        S'empressa de lui crier :

    « Qui vous colle une étiquette
        Peine à vous la dégommer. »

THE SLOTH AND THE LABEL

In Paris's Jardin des Plantes one night,
A supine sloth, eyes heaven-raised, caught sight
Of a star shooting past, and wished on it
As one will do in such a case. To wit,
That "lazy," "slothful" cease forthwith to be
The adjectives that universally
Cling to him… Staunch, he treats the swinging trees
Like balance-rings, parallel bars, trapeze…

       His efforts, vain!

Today, tomorrow, will the sloth remain
"A toothless mammal" that the dictionary
    Defines him as… And "lazy"? Very!
    Cries weasel, watching him:

            "Let's face it.
    Once there's a label stuck on you,
    You'll try your damnedest! All you do
    Is never able to erase it!"

LE SCORPION ET LA SCOLOPENDRE

Dans la septième galerie,
Au lieu-dit « La Souche pourrie »,
Un scorpion était cordonnier.
Il ressemelait les souliers
Et vendait des patins maison,
Patins à glace et à roulettes
A des scarabées, des frelons
Et à des cigales coquettes.
Un beau jour, une scolopendre
Pénètre droit dans l'atelier.
Elle demande au cordonnier :
« As-tu mille chaussons à vendre,
Un chausson souple demi-pointe
Orné de fleurs de coloquinte ? »
Le scorpion sitôt se morfond.
Où trouver autant de chaussons ?
« Je sais que tu es mille-pattes,
Lui explique-t-il, soupçonneux.
Mais si je te compte les pattes,
Je n'en vois que quarante-deux. »
Humiliée, notre scolopendre,
A qui pourtant nul ne veut nuire,
Quitte le lieu sans plus attendre
Pour ne jamais y revenir.

La vérité, par ouï-dire,
N'est pas toujours bonne à entendre.

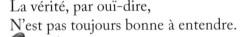

THE SCORPION AND
THE MILLIPEDE

In a boutique, chic as can be,
In the village of Rotting Tree,
A scorpion-cobbler plied his trade,
Re-soling shoes, and sold homemade
Ice skates and roller skates, to boot,
To wasps and beetles, and to cute
Lady cicadas… One fine day,
A scolopendrine creature—nay,
A millipede (easier to say!)—
Comes his way, tells him: "Friend, I need
Slippers… A thousand, if you please—
Flexible, half-toed by the way,
With bitter-apple filigrees…"

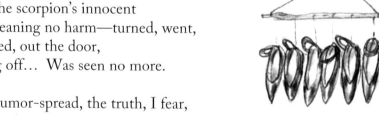

Says Scorpion, scowling, ill at ease:
"I know that you're a millipede,
That 'mille' means 'thousand'. But, indeed,
When I proceed to count your feet,
Unless I frequently repeat
And count some twice, I only come
To forty-eight!" The bug, struck dumb—
Despite the scorpion's innocent
Intent, meaning no harm—turned, went,
Humiliated, out the door,
Slithering off… Was seen no more.

Though rumor-spread, the truth, I fear,
Is seldom what one wants to hear.

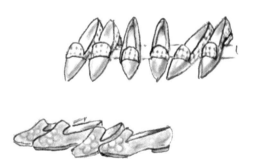

LA GRENOUILLE ET LE BŒUF

Un bœuf apprit par une pie
Qu'une grenouille sans-souci
Voulait entrer dans sa famille,
Fuir la mare pour la prairie
Et être aussi grosse que lui.
Le bœuf ne fut pas enchanté
Par ce souhait peu ordinaire.
Il dit à la pie cancanière :
  « Même si j'apprécie, l'été,
Sur le plateau des nénuphars,
Les concertos du crépuscule
Et le tourbillon des têtards,
Je trouve plutôt désolant
Qu'un batracien si minuscule
Veuille égaler un ruminant.
C'est comme si, à votre tour,
Vous vous preniez pour un vautour. »
La pie se surprit à rêver
Qu'elle était changée en rapace.
Aussi se mit-elle à planer
Gracieusement dans l'espace.
Ce voyant, le bœuf se jucha
Avec la fierté d'un prélat
Sur l'abreuvoir de pierre bleue
Et devant la pie, la grenouille
Saisies, ébahies, à quia,
Le bovidé émit le vœu
D'être transmué en gargouille,
En gargouille phénoménale
Sur un fronton de cathédrale.

Laissons aux rêves leur aura,
En rire serait immoral.

THE FROG AND THE OX

A magpie told an ox that she
Knew of a frog who eagerly
Would join the bovine family,
Leave pond behind, go roaming free
In pasture-dwellers' company,
As big as ox that ever was!
The ox, aghast, hardly rejoicing
At the desire said frog was voicing—
Untoward!—replied: "Ah! Just because,
Dear chatterbox, I hear with pleasure
The summer-twilight frogs perform
Their dusk-concertos, with a swarm
Of tadpoles wriggling round, yet must
I view this wee batrachian's lust
Absurd! Imagine that! To be—
She, a mere frog—as big as me!
As if you, born a magpie, thought
Yourself a vulture misbegot!…"
His words set her a-dreaming… Lo!
Turned her to predator! Why not?
And gracefully our pie will go
Off to space, gliding, soaring high,
Swooping low… Ox too, by and by,
Squats on the blue stone fountain, posing,
Proud, prelate-like (though not quite dozing)
Statue… As, nonplussed, frog and pie
Look on, he yearns before their eye
To become a magnificent
Gargoyle, cathedral-ornament…

Yield to the auras your dreams spin
To lure you on. Deny, defy,
Or laugh at them? That, friend, is sin.

59

LES ESCARGOTS ET LA FEUILLE

Vingt-et-un escargots blancs
Pique-niquent dans un champ.
De la terre sort une feuille.
Les pique-niqueurs l'accueillent,
Se placent tous autour d'elle.
L'un d'eux qui la trouve belle
Veut en faire un char à voile.
Un second, plus terre-à-terre,
Préfère, à rebrousse-poil,
Pencher pour une salade
Jus d'olive et citron vert.
Quelques-uns l'en dissuadent.
« Pas question que l'on me cueille
Comme une menthe, un cerfeuil !
Pas question que je sois voile
Ni salade provençale !
Crie la feuille aux deux benêts.
J'ai droit à ma liberté
Comme tout être vivant
Allez consulter le Code !
C'est dedans écrit en grand.
— Elle a raison pour le Code.
Témoignons-lui du respect.
Dit un vieux gastéropode.

THE SNAILS AND THE LEAF

Twenty-one white snails, in a field,
Have come to have a picnic outing, *
When there, before their eyes, revealed,
A solitary leaf is sprouting.
One and all, finding it quite fit
For many a use, they crawl, plod, slither
Over the ground… Arriving thither,
Pondering on its fate, they sit…
Suggest… Expound… One would turn it
Into a glider-sail… A second,
More down to earth—contrary!—reckoned
That it would be a treat if they
Tossed it, with olive oil and lime,
Into a salad, dinnertime,
For the most elegant gourmet…
"Plucked like a mint-leaf? Nay," she cries,
Finding, in fact, both thoughts abhorrent!
"I would not fancy a demise
As *salade provençale* or sail!"
And to both sots she pleads her cause:
"Like every living thing, I warrant,
I have my rights! I fear you fail
　　　To learn our laws!
Consult the Code!…" They do… Each clause

Il pleut ! Le temps est superbe.
Allons déjeuner sur l'herbe. »
Et chacun de repartir
Sitôt la décision prise
Laissant la feuille grandir,
     A sa guise.

Rules clearly in her favor. Whence,
"Let us show her the deference
That she is due," an elderly
Gasteropod exclaims. And he,
          After a pause,
Continues: "Look! It's raining... We
Couldn't ask for more perfect weather!
Let's have our picnic." All agree...
Our snails, a-nod, crawl off together,
Leaving the leaf to grow... Until
          She grows her fill.

---

* *"Escargot blanc,"* a name given to a number of different types of snail, is
   especially applied to small garden pests common to the Mediterranean
   regions, that characteristically form into clusters and cling to plant stems.
   When asked if he chose the specific number twenty-one for a reason, the
   author replied that he merely wanted an odd number to avoid a tie in the
   scenario's deliberations.

LA TORTUE ET LES COPIEURS

Au parlement des animaux
    De la forêt
    De Rambouillet,
Une tortue, à la tribune,
A clamé haut son infortune :
« On loue partout dans l'univers
Le rôle des panneaux solaires.
Nul ne dit que ma carapace
Fut copiée de pile et de face
Par les prétendus inventeurs.
Debout, mes frères et mes sœurs
Et crions, hurlons, ululons,
Bramons à tous les horizons
Ce que nous doivent les humains,
Ce que pour eux sont chats et chiens,
Et les oiseaux et les chevaux
Et tous les cobayes de labo.
Que les perroquets, les aras
Nous prêtent leurs ailes, leur voix! »
La tortue fut très applaudie
Par une assemblée en folie.
Dès que les bravos s'éteignirent,
Un tout tout petit écureuil
Perché sur les bois d'un chevreuil
S'écria : « J'ai une question,
Une question qui m'interpelle :
Après l'orage, l'arc-en-ciel,
L'arc-en-ciel que nous admirons
N'est-il qu'un faux caméléon ? »

THE TURTLE AND THE COPIERS

In the forest of Rambouillet,
At the animal parliament,
    Turtle, intent
      To have her say,
Rose to the rostrum and proclaimed
That most chagrined was she, and shamed
By the gross, crass indignity
She suffers: "Every day, we're told
The new solar technology
Must be respected, prized, extolled.
But never do its proud inventors,
Anywhere in their solar annals,
Admit—to champions or dissenters—
That, much admired, their solar panels
Were inspired by my carapace!
Rise up, my brothers, sisters! Let
Our cries condemn my pride's disgrace!
Let us shout far and wide the debt
Mankind owes horses, dogs, and cats!
Even the laboratory rats! *
Let the macaws and parrots lend
Their wings, their voices!..." In the end,
Wildly, the proletariat's
Minions applaud her rants... When all
The cheers and chants have died, a small
Squirrel, perched on a horned buck-deer,
Takes the floor: "Comrades mine... Here, here !
A pressing question, please!... When, after
The storm, we stand in awe before

La forêt ne fut plus qu'un rire.
A Rambouillet, sous les vivats,
Le cerf président clôtura
La séance du parlement.
Et chacun repartit, content.

The rainbow, is it not a mere
Would-be chameleon, nothing more?"
At that, the forest shakes with laughter.
Huzzahs ring out in Rambouillet.
The buck, parliament president,
Gavels the session said and done.
Deliberations ended, they
All rise… And each and every one
Proceeds to go his way, content.

---

* I ask the reader's indulgence for changing the original guinea pigs to
equally selfless lab rats, with no detriment to the meaning.

LE LOUP ET LA TOILE

Au fond de sa tanière, un loup se désolait
              D'être plus craint qu'aimé.
Il était solitaire mais très évolué.
Sur un ordinateur qu'il avait dérobé,
Il surfait, à toute heure, sous le nom de "Loup Sage,"
Il inondait Twitter d'appels et de messages.
L'ermite y dénonçait les contes et les fables
Où le loup est méchant et partant détestable.
              Sur la Toile, intrigués,
              Des internautes crurent
              Que "Loup Sage" cachait
              Un écolo poète.
              Certains en étant sûrs
              Ont dès lors alerté
              Les médias, coup sur coup,
              Les défenseurs des bêtes
              Et sans tarder, le loup
              Devint, en quelques clics,
              Animal sympathique.
Au temps des satellites et des clés USB,
Je sais que cette histoire est difficile à croire
              Et même à répéter.
Ou alors on se dit que, loup ermite ou pas,
Vaincre l'*a priori* n'est pas un vain combat.

THE WOLF AND THE INTERNET

A wolf—a hermit, though quite up to date—
      Deep in his lair, appeared
Distressed—obsessed!—by wolfdom's common fate.
Distraught, alas, to be not loved but feared!
On his computer (no doubt stolen) he
Would surf day long, "Sly Wolf," his Twitter name…
In blog and e-mail, keying constantly,
He would defend his kind, quick to proclaim
Hateful and false those tales and fables that
Defame the wolf; and, giving tit for tat,
Would do his best to cleanse his race of shame.
      Many an Internaut—
      Intrigued Net-surfers—thought
      That "Sly Wolf" marked some very
      Earth-concerned poet, some
      Ecolo-luminary;
      And they, *ad libitum,*
      Informed the press, TV,
      And all the company
      Of animal befrienders
      And Wildlife Rights defenders.
With just a few keyboard clicks, now and then,
Wolf, once much loathed, turned honest citizen.
      I know this apologue
Will be met with far fewer "ayes" than "nays"!
But, with "flash drives" and satellites these days,
Be the wolf pleasant chap or hermit rogue,
It's worth the effort to pooh-pooh clichés.

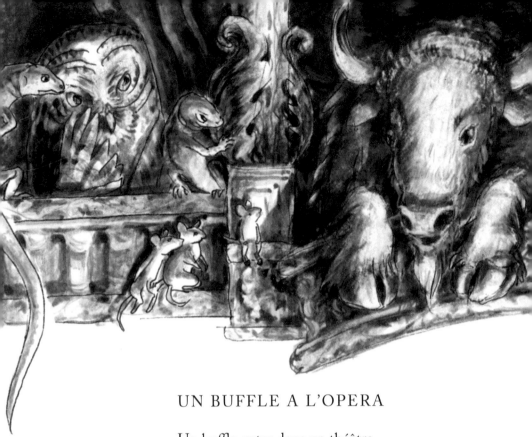

UN BUFFLE A L'OPERA

Un buffle entra dans un théâtre
On y jouait un opéra.
En avant-scène, une marâtre
Vocalisait à pleine voix.
Sans bruit, le buffle pénétra
Dans une loge inoccupée
Riche en velours et en dorures.
L'opéra avait belle allure.
L'intrus aussitôt fut charmé
Par le plateau bien décoré.
Il applaudit les envolées,
Les grands airs de la tragédie,
La grâce des chorégraphies
Et crut bon, d'une voix martiale,
D'entonner l'hymne national.
Le public se leva d'un bond
Et se tourna, interloqué,

A BUFFALO AT THE OPERA

A buffalo had found his way
Into a theater where, that day,
Opera was on the bill of fare.
Thereupon, quietly, the beast—
While a large harridan-artiste
(I swear!), regaling the *parterre*
Downstage, was loudly ululating
Before the lights, arpeggiating—
Finding a box unoccupied,
Slipped in among the lush excess,
All gold and silk arrayed inside.
Charmed by the tragic tale's bravura—
The elegant terpsichore,
The graceful choreography,
The set, props, costumes and, no less,
By the diva's coloratura—
He thought it fitting to express

Vers la loge du roi Lion
Que le buffle prenait pour sienne.
La salle hua l'énergumène
Qui profanait le lieu sacré
Et laissa monter sa colère.
Ce voyant, notre patriote
Préféra filer, ventre à terre,
Avant qu'un ouvreur l'emmenotte.
Ce qu'il advint de cet intrus,
Personne ne l'a jamais su.

S'il sied de louer le mérite,
L'admiration a ses limites.

His admiration with applause,
Intoning in most military
Manner, "La Marseillaise"!… This very
Awkward reaction draws guffaws
Of awe. The public gapes and gawks,
Stares at King Lion's royal box:
The very one, in fact, that was
The box our patriot ox was in!
Whereat much angry roar and din…
Our lout—midst many an outraged shout
Damning the profanation wrought
This day upon this sacred spot!—
Slinks off lest he be ushered out
In shackles!… So the story goes.
What next? Alas, nobody knows.

But clear it is: when earned, our praise
Ought be expressed in modest ways.

LE PAPEGAI ET LA MOUCHETTE

« Je connais le secret
Du Soleil qui se couche,
Dit une jeune mouche,
Un tantinet pédante
A un vieux papegai
Suçotant une menthe.
Quand la nuit tombe ici,
Le jour se lève ailleurs.
Le soleil, à toute heure,
N'est jamais dans son lit.
— A mon tour, un secret !
Répond le papegai.
Sais-tu pourquoi, Jeunette,
La girafe est muette ? »
La mouchette, baba,
Admet son ignorance
De ce mystère-là,
En exige la clef,
Non sans quelque impatience.
Le papegai se tait.
A l'instant, un colvert
Que la pédante agace
S'élève dans les airs
Et sur ce, lui jacasse :

« Un secret ne se dit pas.
Cherche et tu le trouveras ! »

THE PARROT POPINJAY AND
THE LITTLE FLY

A minuscule young fly—
A pedant, she—cries, "Oh!"
To parrot-popinjay,
Sipping his *menthe à l'eau.*
"I know a secret... Why
The sun dips from the sky!
When night falls here, the day
Dawns somewhere else instead:
Sun never goes to bed!"
"I know a secret too,"
Replies the popinjay.
"Tell me, dear child, do you
Know why our friend giraffe
Can neither cry nor laugh,
Nor say the merest word?"
The fly gapes at our bird:
Too deep this mystery!
And she, impatiently,
Demands the facts be heard...
A mallard happens by,
Hearing the pedant-fly—
Who raises high his hackles!—
And, soaring to the sky,
Leering at her, he cackles:

"A secret hides a truth behind it.
Seek for yourself if you would find it!"

LE POISSON-CHAT ET LA SOURIS

Un poisson-chat malappris
Rencontra une souris.
Il paria cent puces d'eau
  Qu'à midi,
Il dégusterait au chaud
  La souris.
La souris tint le pari
Et le poisson tint parole :
Il avala la bestiole.
Soudain mis en appétit,
Un héron rôdant par là
Becqueta le poisson-chat
Et digéra la souris.
Restent les cent puces d'eau :
Elles rient dans les roseaux.

Qui parie pour un enjeu
Se doit de cacher son jeu.

THE CATFISH AND THE MOUSE

A catfish—a *méchant esprit*—
Happens upon a mouse, and he
        Casually shrugs,
Bets her a hundred water-bugs
        That, come noon, she
Will be a tasty fricassee.
The mouse is quick to take the bet,
Whereat the catfish, one two three,
Gobbles her up, no fuss, no fret…
A passing heron, hungrily
Watching the scene, likewise makes free,
Gluts on both fish and rodentlet!
The hundred water-bugs? Still there,
Reed-bound, mocking the whole affair…

When you would bet, best understand:
Better you not go tip your hand.

LE TAUREAU ET LE TORERO

Un taureau entra dans l'arène
Avec la cape et le chapeau,
Une pique entre les naseaux.
Selon un journal madrilène,
L'animal respecta, sans mal,
Devant les aficionados,
Le salut, le cérémonial
Puis affronta le torero.
Celui-ci ne s'attendait guère
A combattre un tel adversaire.
Lors, devant des gradins debout,
Il prit ses jambes à son cou.
Sur la toile, tout aussitôt,
Des Bobos se firent l'écho
De la honte du torero.
Indignés, l'un voulut la tête,
L'autre une oreille de la bête

THE BULL AND THE TOREADOR

A bull entered the bullring, dressed
In cap and cape, a spike betwixt
His nostrils, properly affixed.
A paper—Madrid's newsiest—
Reported that, with due respect,
Much to the joy of the fanatics,
The animal, richly bedecked,
Indulging in bull acrobatics,
Bowed to Señor Torero, who
Never suspected he would be
Forced to face such-like enemy!
Whereat, thereon, and thereunto,
Before the stands, rising to see
What he would do, he hurriedly
Turned tail, ran, fled the scene!… Now then,
Many a Madrid denizen—
Limp bourgeois "metrosexual"— *

Sans penser que cette semaine,
Au sein du journal madrilène,
La fausse info est tombée pile
Le matin du premier avril.

En ces temps dits de vérité,
Sans borne est la crédulité.

Shocked at the details textual,
Beset the Net, aghast, agog,
With deluge of e-mail and blog
Against the shamed toreador,
And claimed the head of Don Señor.
Others railed at the beast and sought
At least the *toro's* ear… None thought
That this concocted story burst
Upon the scene on April first!

In these days, when truth ought hold sway,
Limitless is man's *naïveté*.

---

* I translate with an American neologism of the early '90s the equally
rather recent French coinage "Bobo," referring to a bourgeois would-be
Bohemian. The latter was introduced by David Brooks in his *Bobos in
Paradise* (2000), and has since been spread by popular French singer
Renaud (Séchan) in his song "Les Bobos."

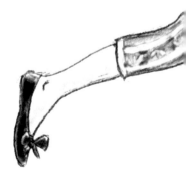

L'EXPLORATEUR ET LE LION

Il s'acheta un fauve
Et le peignit en vert.
Il se para de mauve
Et courut l'univers.
On ne s'étonna guère.
Lorsque l'explorateur
Rentra fourbu, moulu
De son lointain périple,
Il fut avalé cru
Par son bestial disciple.
Trop peu s'en étonnèrent.
Quand le lion sans honneur
Mais non sans appétit
Fut abattu dans l'heure
Et en catimini,
Certains s'en étonnèrent.
Sur les réseaux sociaux,
Au nom des animaux,
Des furieux dénoncèrent
L'humaine cruauté.

A chacun sa moralité.

THE EXPLORER AND THE LION

He bought a lion that
He painted green, and he,
Decked out in mauve… Whereat,
Explorer and said cat
Roamed the world, roving free…
When home he comes—worn out
From gadding roundabout—
No one spouts righteous awe
To see his pupil feast
On him, and eat him raw!
Some, though, pity the beast,
Distressed—distraught—to see
Man's needless cruelty:
Poor hungry creature! Why,
Assassin on the sly,
Kill him summarily?
"Animal rights!" they cry,
Ranting, bolder and bolder…

Morality is in the eye
        Of the beholder.

LE CHAT ET LA LUNE

Juché sur le crâne de pierre
D'une statue de Jupiter,
Un chat miaulait à la Lune :
« Dame, je plains votre infortune,
Vous qui ne cessez de tourner,
Tourner de face et de profil
Autour du Soleil immobile.
Refusez de tournicoter.
Contentez-vous de réguler
Le va-et-vient de vos marées ! »
Muet, comme chacun le sait,
L'astre lunaire, interpellé,
Dépêche vers le chat perché,
Son oiseau de mer préféré.
« Oubliez-vous que notre Terre
Tourne depuis des millénaires,
Crie le goéland messager,
Et que dès lors, sans le vouloir,
Vous tournez du matin au soir ? »
A ces mots, la tête en émoi,
Pris de vertige, le chat choit
Et sur-le-champ fuit Jupiter,
La Lune et son oiseau de mer.

Qui compatit se doit d'avoir
A tout le moins de la mémoire.

84

THE CAT AND THE MOON

On the god Jupiter (on his
Stone skull)—on his statue, that is—
Gazing up at the Moon, there sat,
Perched, a most sympathetic cat,
Meowing: "Madame, distressed am I
At your misfortune. For I see
How you must turn—eternally,
Full face or profile, by the by—
About the Sun, set in the sky,
Motionless… You should simply say:
'An end to my travail! Nay, nay!
Enough!' You could be satisfied
To be the mistress of the tide—
Its rising and its falling…" Mutely,
The orb dispatches to the cat
Her seabird most preferred. Whereat,
Squawks messenger-gull resolutely:
"Do you forget, I wonder, that,
We, on our earthly habitat,
Thousands of years, morning and night,
Go wandering round as well, not one
Whit less, about the selfsame sun?"
His words dizzy our feline, quite,
Who topples from Jupiter's skull,
Despite himself, flees god and gull,
Ignoring the distressing crisis,
Leaving the Moon to her devices.

Be sympathetic. But your disposition
Shouldn't let you forget your own condition.

LE CHIEN ET L'OISEAU

Un grand chien a caché son os
Dans un terrain rempli de bosses.
L'ennui, c'est qu'il ne sait plus où,
Où est son os, où est le trou.
Le distrait est très en colère,
Il aboie, se traîne par terre,
Maudit le ciel et Lucifer.
« Hé ! Ton os, je l'ai découvert
En cherchant des graines, des vers
Pour mon déjeuner du matin,
Je te le rends. Calme-toi, chien !
Lui crie un petit moineau gris.
Chez nous comme chez les humains,
Les grands ont besoin des petits. »

THE DOG AND THE BIRD

A dog buries his bone. The hound's
Hiding-place is a field with mounds
All roundabout, and he cannot,
Alas, recall tittle or jot
That might reveal the very spot.
Chagrined, the absentminded cur
Grows angrier and angrier…
Barks… Curses heaven—and Lucifer!…
A swallow twitters: "Shhh, monsieur!
That bone you buried? Here, I found it,
Scratching for worms and seeds around it,
Looking for breakfast!"
                      Swallow? Hound? It
Proves this truth: Men and beasts? We all
Need one another, great or small.

LE BOUC ET L'IMAGE

Changer d'image ne suffit pas
Si l'esprit reste terre-à-terre
Comme le montre, de ce pas,
Un bouc qui croyait le contraire.

Pour épater la galerie,
Un bouc a suivi un régime,
Régime à basses calories.
Lorsque la cure s'acheva,
Les avis furent unanimes.
Le rondouillard ne l'était plus.
Il fit la une des médias,
Joua bientôt les m'as-tu-vu
Puis annonça que désormais,
Il ferait de la politique,
Ce qu'il fit dénonçant l'excès
Des obèses, des faméliques
Selon lui, bien trop paresseux
Pour choisir le juste milieu.
Devenu peuple attitré,
Il fréquenta, comme il devait,
Cocktails, apéros dînatoires.
Sa balance reprit espoir.
La presse alors le laissa choir.
Le bouc, seul, en mal de suffrages
Se dit victime des sondages
Et résigné, tourna la page.

THE GOAT AND HIS IMAGE

Wit matters more than image, though
Goat needed life to show him so.

A goat heard of a slimming diet:
Very low-calorie. It would,
Thought he, be well for him to try it,
For he was hopeful that it could
Impress his public! And, when thus
The said regime was duly done,
The verdict was unanimous:
"A butterball no more!" Each one
Agreed. And he decreed that he
Would make a documentary
To publicize the regimen…
Our glamorous goat decided then
On a political career,
To battle both obesity
And hunger. "For people, I fear,
Are lazy, and won't persevere
To ply a middle course. Too fat,
Too thin…" Now a celebrity,
He attends cocktails, fetes, whereat
He gluts his fill… Till, once again—
His diet dead and gone (amen!)—
Once more a butterball, he tops
The scales… The press now promptly drops
All talk of him. His campaign, shaken,
And by the voters fast forsaken,
He blames the polls ("They did me in!"),
Turns the page on what might have been…

LE CRABE ET LES COQUILLAGES

Au bout de la jetée,
Tourné vers l'Orient,
Un crabe méditait.
Du large, un coup de vent
Le fit soudain rouler
Parmi des coquillages
Rosés, dorés, nacrés
Qui bruitaient sur la plage.
Il écouta longtemps
Les coquilles sans vie
Qui néanmoins chantaient.
A l'heure où le jour fuit
Comme à la dérobée,
Le crabe, impressionné
Par ce marin mystère,
Regagna la jetée
Et là-haut, en voyant
Des mollusques vivants
Collés à une pierre
Leur dit, comme à regret :
    « Il est dommage
     Qu'un coquillage
Ne chante pas la mer
Lorsqu'il est habité. »

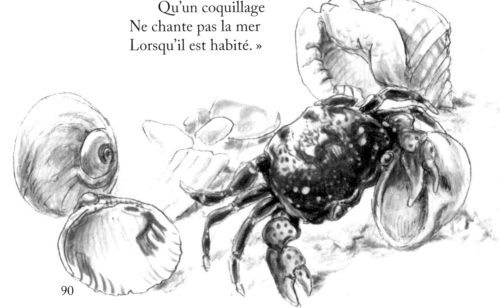

THE CRAB AND THE SHELLS

In meditation lying,
A crab faced toward the East,
At jetty's edge. Come flying,
A gust sweeps the poor beast
Onto the shells below—
Pink-pearled, deep gold, aglow—
Whistling there on the beach…
With ear long pressed to each
Cockle-shell—lifeless now
But which, though empty, dead,
Still sings its song—he said,
Wondering, amazed: "Pray, how
Explain this mystery?…"
As day, with stealthy tread,
Turns and begins to flee,
Once more he scales the jetty,
Spies a rock… With regret, he
Sees clinging to it there,
A mollusk colony,
Alive but mute… "I swear!
         Too bad!
         How sad
      That one must be
An empty shell to sing the sea!"

LA LANGOUSTE ET LA MANGOUSTE

Une langouste, une mangouste
Participaient au festival
De musique interanimale.
Elles furent les invitées
D'une émission télévisée.
« Je suis timbalier, dit la langouste.
— Je suis cymbalier, dit la mangouste. »
Le présentateur, un mandrill,
Cynocéphale prétentieux,
Soucieux de son meilleur profil,
D'entrée, crut bon de demander :

THE CRAYFISH AND THE MONGOOSE

A musical symposium—
A celebrated festival
Of music inter-animal—
Takes place in France. To it have come
A crayfish (in French, a *langouste*)
And a mongoose (ditto, *mangouste*),
That some would-be celebrity
(Some dog-faced mandrill), on TV,
Interviews live and unrehearsed.
"I play guitar," proclaims the first
In Langouste tongue, freely translated.

« Vos deux noms créent la confusion.
Nombreux sont ceux qui par le monde
Vous méconnaissent, vous confondent.
J'avoue que j'étais parmi eux.
— Ravie je suis, dit la mangouste,
De mettre fin à l'ignorance
Qui fut vôtre depuis l'enfance. »
Ce qui ne plut guère au mandrill
Qui reprit sur un ton hostile :
« Avec vos timbale et cymbale
Les instruments dont vous jouez,
Vous doublez notre confusion.
Trouvez-vous tout cela normal ?
— Absolument ! crie la langouste.
Je suis avant tout musicienne.
Si mon nom prête à confusion
Avec celui de ma consœur,
Sans hésiter, quoi qu'il advienne,
Cherchez l'âne et trouvez l'erreur. »
Le crustacé pince-sans-rire
Ajouta après un soupir :
« Tout est dit ! Sur ce, je propose
Que nous devisions d'autre chose. »
Il en fut ainsi, c'est logique :
On parla enfin de musique

"I play sitar." exclaims the second
In Mangouste, similarly stated. *
"I've always thought... I've always reckoned...
Assumed..." stammers the prig M.C.,
Careful to show the camera
His better side... "I... Ah..."
And he continues: "Actually...
Your names, I mean... They're rather... Well,
Confusing... Difficult to tell
Apart... For many... Even me!"
Scorns Mongoose: "Glad to disabuse you,
Ignorant ape, and un-confuse you!"
Which observation, our mandrill,
Tact to the winds, takes rather ill,
Saying: "And now, to add insult
To injury, you tell us what
You play—sitar, guitar—which but
Compounds—confounds!—the end result!"
The Crayfish sneers: "Monsieur, tut-tut!
It matters little how obtuse is
My name for you, or friend Mongoose's!
I'm a musician... So is he.
So fiddlesticks and fiddle-de-dee!
Go find a stupid jackass who
No doubt will know more than you do!"
And, with a note of indignation,
Sighing, the tongue-in-cheek crustacean
Adds: "Now there's nothing more to say!"
Mandrill, Mongoose, and Crayfish... They,
Recalling why they're there, the three
Talk about music... Finally!

---

* The reader will, I hope, understand my liberties and specific diver-
 gences from the original's details, imposed by its intricate wordplay.
 Case in point: the instruments mentioned.

LE LION ET LE GORILLE

Un roi vivait tranquille
A cent lieues de la ville
En son riche palais.
C'était un lion sage
Aimé de l'entourage
Et de ses conseillers.
Comme il prenait de l'âge,
Il engage à prix d'or
Un vrai garde du corps,
Gorille haut et fort :
Costard de va-t-en-guerre,
iPad et revolver.

THE LION AND THE GORILLA

A king dwelt peacefully
In palace luxury.
Twenty leagues from the town.
Lion much loved was he
For his sagacity,
By all pledged to the Crown—
His courtly retinue.
But as the monarch grew
Longish of tooth, he thought
Best that His Majesty—
On royal introspection,
Considering his lot—

Bientôt, chacun se terre
Tant le garde est sévère.
Le roi sort, il le suit.
Le roi dort, il le veille
Du coucher à l'éveil
Et sans le moindre bruit.
Privé de liberté,
Le monarque regrette
Le temps où il pouvait
Se rendre où il voulait
Sans qu'un œil ne le guette.
Et sur ce, par sagesse,
Sire Lion s'empresse
De remercier le garde
Et d'opter sans regret
Pour une vie peinarde
En son riche palais.

Que les rois le veuillent ou non,
Le protocole est leur prison,
    Et leur barbouze
    Une ventouse
    Sans voix ni nom.

Engage proper protection.
Which he did… For a fee
Outlandish, he acquired
The services of one
Gorilla-hulk (with gun
And iPad!), promptly hired…
Everyone, cowed with fear,
Was careful to steer clear
Of martial ape, who never
Left the king's side, forever
Hovering… Ever there,
Inside and out… Awake,
Asleep… Prepared to take
Action should ill betide…
Until the king could bear
No more, nor more abide
His eyes' incessant stare…
He sighs, yearns for escape!
And so he fires the ape,
Returns, devil-may-care,
To idle liberty
Of palace luxury!

Protocol is kings' prison—barred,
        Shut tight—and each
Silent-tongued gumshoe bodyguard,
        Anonymous,
        A bloody leech!…
        ('Twas ever thus.)

LA CRECERELLE CANTATRICE

Une très jolie crécerelle
Voulait devenir cantatrice,
Diva que des fans applaudissent
Tant ils la croient exceptionnelle.
Elle rêvait d'une tournée,
De chanter *La Flûte enchantée.*
Une audition lui a suffi.
Douze jurés, un seul avis :
Avec une voix de crécelle,
Fût-on faucon ou crécerelle,
Pas question, si l'on s'égosille,
D'être la Reine de la Nuit.
L'oiselle alors dut mettre au clou
Son ambition, son songe fou
Et plus dépitée qu'en colère
Annonça qu'elle choisissait
Désormais le karaoké.
C'est ce qu'il convenait de faire.

THE FALCON-DIVA

Bird of the falcon family—
Petite kestrel by name—she dreamed
That she an opera star might be;
A diva her admirers deemed
Unmatched, and who so peerless was
That they esteemed with wild applause
Her every role. She would have gone
On tour, singing *The Magic Flute.*
Well, one audition… Whereupon,
Twelve judges, one decision: mute
Ought she remain! Her cackling rasp
(Were she to sing "Queen of the Night")
Would cause an opera house to gasp,
Agog, and gag, and faint with fright!
Still, resolute, she'll not let spite
Dash her ambition!… But that voice—
Now shrill, now crackling, hoarse and croaky—
Gives her but one artistic choice.
Yes, now she stars in karaoke.

LA BELETTE ET LE FURET

Une belette et un furet
En tête-à-tête conversaient
Sur le versant sale à souhait
D'une bretelle d'autoroute.
« Avouez que c'est désolant
Ce lieu qui dégoutte et dégoûte !
Se plaint la belette en voyant
Les bouteilles et les cannettes,
Les déchets que des humains jettent
De leurs engins pétaradants.
— Ils sont d'une paresse insigne.
Mais gardent ce qui se consigne,
Dénonce, à son tour, le furet.
Ils croient agir en liberté.
C'est la liberté qu'ils profanent. »
Après avoir philosophé
Entre plastique et cellophane,
Les fouineurs mis en appétit
Par les senteurs du restoroute
Décident d'y casser la croûte
Avant de regagner leur antre.

La nourriture de l'esprit
N'altère pas celle du ventre.

THE WEASEL AND THE FERRET

A highway ramp covered with all
Manner of filth spread here and there…
And, crawling on the road, a pair—
Weasel and Ferret—eye the sprawl
Of bottles, cans, and trash; converse
About the grimy, slimy slop.
"Good grief," Weasel exclaims. "What's worse
Than all that junk the humans drop—
Or fling!—from those farting machines
Of theirs!" And, knowing what he means,
Ferret agrees: "Foul, lazy lot!
They think they're free to throw out what
They please!… Almost, that is… Too cheap,
They litter, but make sure to keep
What they've put a deposit on!…"
And on they natter… Whereupon,
After philosophizing thus
On styrofoam, and cellophane,
And piles of vile putridities,
Our burrowing complainers twain—
Growing more and more ravenous
From stench of highway eateries—
Decide that first they'll have a snack,
Then to their den go crawling back.

Food for thought? Feeds the senses, but
Chatter won't feed a hungry gut.

LA TOURISTE ET LES POISSONS

A la criée du littoral,
Une touriste s'extasie
Devant les poissons d'un étal.
« Quelle fraîcheur ! Quelle beauté !
Et quelle parfaite harmonie ! »
S'exclame-t-elle au poissonnier
Qui la trouve un peu théâtrale
D'autant qu'elle n'achète rien.
Il se fait que la dame tient
Dans un petit sac en plastique
Deux poissons rouges frénétiques
Plus agités que sémaphores.
Tous deux sont d'un avis contraire
Face au poissonneux cimetière.
« La vie est belle, pas la mort,
Dit le premier. Alors, fuyons !
— Tu as raison, dit le second.
Passer ma vie dans un bocal
Ne me paraît plus l'idéal. »
            Et dare-dare,
            Ils font des bonds,
            Tournent en rond
Si follement que le sac
                Craque
Et se vide dans l'eau du port,
Laissant le poissonnier hilare
Et la touriste sans ressort
Devant l'étal des poissons morts.

A la fin d'une heureuse issue,
Toute morale est superflue.

THE TOURIST LADY AND THE FISH

A tourist market at the shore,
And there, a fancy pet fish store…
Gazing, awed, at the realm aquatic,
Before a tank, waxing ecstatic,
A lady revels: "Mercy me!
How beautiful! Such harmony,
Such grace!…" The shop's proprietor,
Finds her to be a bit dramatic—
Irksome, in fact… And, all the more,
Because she had, apparently,
Purchased from some competitor
A pair of goldfish in a plastic
Sack, swimming in a frenzy spastic,
Zigzagging in their helplessness,
And who pooh-poohed the lady, very
Scornful of their fish cemetery!
"Beautiful?" said the first… "Life? Yes…
But death? Alas, a good deal less!…
Let's escape!" "Let's!" the second said.
"Frankly, I'd rather we were dead
Than spend life in a bowl!" So saying,
      Round, round… Forth, back…
      The pair attack
The plastic sack, instinct obeying,
Until, under their fierce attacks,
      It cracks…
And, as the water joins the tide,
Proprietor, now satisfied,
Smiles at the tourist, there, before
Her fish, quite dead, and hers no more.

As with all happy endings, thus,
A moral is superfluous.

LA CHEVRE ET LE BASSET

Sur un marché du voisinage,
Une chèvre vend ses fromages.
Devant le stand, cette biquette
Présente aux passants une assiette
Garnie de cubes à goûter.
A pleine voix, la chèvre bêle :
« Je vous invite à déguster
Mes produits en toute confiance.
Ils sont cent pour cent naturels
Et conformes à vos exigences. »
Un basset soudain l'interpelle,
Le seul journaliste à temps plein
D'une radio libre du coin.
Il traite la chèvre de haut :
« Pourquoi ne pas vivre en troupeau
Comme la plupart de vos sœurs
Ont, de tout temps, pris l'habitude ?
Pourquoi choisir de vivre ailleurs ?
— Le troupeau, c'est la servitude

THE NANNY GOAT AND THE BASSET HOUND

Neighborhood market… Open-air…
A nanny goat is selling there
Her home-made cheese. Before her stand,
Our dairy-goat, with plate in hand—
"In hoof," that is—holds out to all
The curious passers-by, her small
Samples, cut into cubes, to try…
She offers, hawks with throaty cry:
"Come, taste my cheese… I promise you
It's made with pure milk, nature's own!…
Best grains and grass!… The finest grown!…
Hundred percent organic too!…"
All at once, looms up, thereupon,
A basset hound, figure well-known—
The only full-time anchor on
A private local radio station.
Scorning haughty goat's ostentation,
"Why not," he asks, "live in a flock
Like all your sister goats?" "Don't talk!"

107

A un berger et à un chien,
Et la nuit, c'est la solitude
Dans un enclos, une clairière.
Croyez-moi, ce n'est pas commode
Quand d'aventure, un renard rôde,
Lui réplique la fromagère.
Sous un abri proche d'un puits,
Loin des cabots et des goupils,
Poursuit-elle avec bonhomie,
Je prends mon temps et je le gère
Sans qu'un seul intrus n'intervienne.
Ma liberté est ma gardienne.
Sur ce, goûtez une corolle
De mon crottin de Chavignol ! »
Il n'est certes pas coutumier
Que sur la place du marché,
Vous invite et vous apostrophe
Une caprine philosophe.

Says she. "A flock means sequestration
And bondage to shepherd and hound!
At night, it's cooped up in a pen,
Or in the meadow, lolling round…
Believe me, it's no pleasure then,
When fox prowls roundabout… When death
Stealthily stalks your final breath!"
So says the nanny goat. And she
Adds, with a note of *bonhomie:*
"Rather would I stop, spend a spell
Safely beside a nearby well,
Un-hounded and un-foxed, where, free
To come and go, my liberty
Saves me from danger's vagaries…
Here, my friend! Have a chunk of cheese…" *
Unusual, you would concur:
A market-place, spouting the quote—
Deep, no doubt—of a nanny goat,
Playing the sage philosopher!

---

* *Crottin de Chavignol* is a much-prized goat cheese from the small Loire-valley town of Chavignol. The etymology of the first part of its name is dubious, though some insist that it derives from the hard consistency of aged Chavignol, resembling a sheep dropping—a *crottin* (from *crotte,* animal dung)—which does not, however, deter its many enthusiasts.

LE LION QUI FUT ROI

Un lion du Zimbabwe
Vieux à n'avoir plus d'âge
Vivait depuis des lustres
Et en bon voisinage
A la cité lacustre
D'un parc animalier.
Il avait été roi,
Un roi puissant mais sage
Qui respectait les lois,
Les droits et les usages.
Ceux qui l'avaient connu
Lui restaient attachés
Et louaient ses vertus.
Maints autres l'ignoraient
Ou ne s'en souciaient guère.
Certains même moquaient
Ce sire solitaire
A la vie monotone,
Ce souverain d'hier
Et à présent déchu.
Le lion en souffrait
Mais n'inquiétait personne.
Au parc, un moyen duc,
Hibou en résidence
Bouboule à l'assistance,
De l'hyène au zébu :
« Avoir une perruque
Après une couronne,

THE LION WHO HAD BEEN KING

By a lake in the veldt—
Wildlife preserve—there dwelt
Ex-king Zimbabwean:
Lion… Good neighbor, he.
Beast passing elderly,
Beyond the age of Man,
Older than time he was.
Respecter of the laws,
Powerful—yes!—but wise
And virtuous… Still admired
And honored in the eyes
Of his ex-subjects, and
Still loved throughout the land.
Now, at long last, retired…
Many there are who never
Give the least thought whatever
To what he once had been.
Much to the beast's chagrin,
Some leer, with mocking hiss
And grinning sneer, at this
Monarch of yesteryear,
Uncrowned, and now a mere
Citizen, suffering
In silence… Bored, alone,
Our one-time mighty king
Must give ear to the drone
Of Sire Owl—middling Duke
In Residence—haranguing

C'est le sort des puissants
Qui le furent longtemps
Et qui ne le sont plus.
Les souverains du monde
Ne sont pas éternels. »
— C'est vrai, dit le vieux roi
Sans élever la voix
Mais d'un éclair qui gronde,
Il naît un arc-en-ciel. »

Zebu, hyena, hanging
On every hoot: "When one
Trades crown for mere *perruque*,
Oh! How the mighty fall!
Earth's sovereigns, after all,
Were born to die, undone!"
"True," sighs the agèd king,
In calm, subdued rebuke.
"But when the lightning dies,
And mute its thundering,
A rainbow spans the skies…"

113

LE PAON, LA PAONNE ET LA NOCE

En l'absence des paysans
Partis tôt moissonner leurs champs,
Un paon épousa une paonne.
Devant toute la basse-cour,
Un dindon gloussa un discours
Mais le micro tomba en panne.
Et dès lors, qu'à cela ne tienne,
On demanda à une chienne
D'asperger le couple de riz,
Ce que de bon cœur, elle fit.
Les invités s'en régalèrent.
Une dinde dit un poème,
Un poème d'Apollinaire
Beaucoup trop long, toujours le même,
Si l'on en croit le caneton
Le plus cancanier du domaine.
Après avoir cassé la graine,
Dégusté la tourte au melon,
But l'eau claire de la fontaine,
Et remercié comme il se doit,
Chacun s'en retourna chez soi.
Les époux choisirent la grange
Afin que nul ne les dérange.
Et le domaine cher aux paons
Reprit son train-train comme avant.
De nos jours, il reste des noces
Sans tralala et sans carrosse
Qui gardent leur attrait d'antan.

THE PEACOCK, THE PEAHEN, AND
THE WEDDING

Fall, and the peasants all had gone
Off to the harvest. Whereupon,
A peacock took advantage of
The calm to wed his peahen love.
Honored guests—all the barnyard fowl—
Were in attendance, beak to jowl.
A cackling, gurgling turkey chattered
A speech… Until his microphone
Broke down—it seems a fuse had blown—
But no one cared. It hardly mattered:
He nattered on… They asked a bitch
To toss rice on the couple, which
She did with pleasure, to the great
Delight of all those present… Then
They listened as a turkey hen,
Taking her part in the affair,
Read something from Apollinaire
(A poem of his, one that the duckling—
Nastiest barnyard gossip—chuckling,
Found long and dull…) When, by and by,
At the reception, each partook
Most copiously of melon pie
And water from the nearby brook,
With proper thanks, each goes his way…
The happy couple chose to stay
In the barn, undisturbed… And here,
Once more, the usual, everyday,
Beloved peacock-farm atmosphere…
Though gone the pomp, the carriages—
Today, there are still marriages
With all the charm of yesteryear.

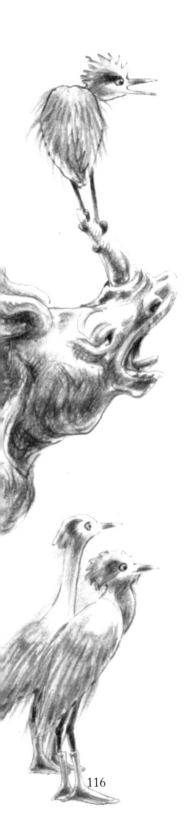

LES DEUX RHINOCEROS

Au zoo, dans la salle d'attente,
Deux gros rhinocéros patientent
Avec un daim et un puma.
Comme souvent en pareil cas,
Certains se taisent, d'autres pas.
« Permettez-moi d'être étonné,
Barrit l'un des rhinos à l'autre.
J'ai une corne sur le nez.
Vous en avez deux sur le vôtre.
Est-ce là une anomalie
Ou une greffe consentie
Pour paraître moins conformiste
Comme le sont nombre d'artistes ? »
Il y eut d'abord un silence
Que ni le daim ni le puma
Ne rompirent par bienséance.
Puis le bicorne s'exclama,
Non sans un soupçon d'ironie :
« Tutoyons-nous, rhinos nous sommes
Egaux tous deux aux yeux des hommes.
Je suis d'Afrique, tu es d'Asie :
C'est ce qui nous différencie.
Ma foi, je ne sais pas pourquoi
J'ai une corne en plus que toi.
Entre encornés, quelle importance !
Sot qui se fie à l'apparence ! »

THE TWO RHINOCEROS

In the zoo's waiting-room, two stout
Rhinoceros are—what else?—waiting…
Other beasts, too, loll roundabout—
Puma, buck—some vociferating,
Some silently… When, with a shout,
One of the rhino pair blares out:
"Permit me, sir, to query you
About a question plaguing me.
One horn have I, as you can see,
Upon my snout, whilst you have two!
Pray tell," he adds, in voice sarcastic,
"Why? Is it some anomaly?
Or the result of rhinoplastic,
Prideful cosmetic surgery,
As practiced on ego-artistes?…"
Respectful silence, as the beasts—
Puma, buck—utter not a peep…
The double-horned exclaims: "Let's keep
A friendly tone… You can't deny
Man sees us both as rhinos: I,
From Africa; from Asia, you. *
No other difference, *entre nous!*
Amongst us who are horn-bedecked,
It doesn't matter, I suspect—
Not a jot, nor the merest tittle!—
How many horns we choose to wear.
Who but a sot would claim to care?
Appearances count precious little!"

* Some readers will recall the lively dispute in Ionesco's short story and
  play, *Rhinocéros,* as the town's inhabitants begin—and continue—to be
  transformed into the pachyderms in question.

LE TIGRE ROYAL ET
LES FELIDES

Avant le banquet qui clôture
Le rendez-vous des Félidés,
Dans son discours, le Président,
Tigre royal de noble allure
Plus mesuré que violent,
Souligna qu'il était malsain,
Malvenu et immérité
Que pour maints humains, les félins
Ne soient que de féroces bêtes
Alors qu'ils sont force et beauté.
Un léopard hocha la tête
Et s'adressa à l'assemblée :
« Vous et moi ne pouvons nier
Qu'en brousse, nous sommes nantis
D'un assez féroce appétit.
Quand nous décimons un troupeau,
Du gibier suivi à la trace,
Ce n'est certes pas un cadeau
Fait à la meute et aux rapaces. »
Un lynx, goguenard, réagit :
« Assez de cris, de bavardages !
Assumons-nous avec courage.
Que chacun, en fier animal,
Brave les chasseurs de tous poils !
Je crois qu'ainsi tout sera dit.
— Si vous vous en sortez vivant,

THE ROYAL TIGER AND
THE FELINE RACE

Before the closing banquet that
Will end the meeting of Cat Nation—
Formal feline association
Serving the worldwide needs of Cat,
Both big and small—the President,
Royal tiger aristocrat,
Beast more gentle than violent,
Makes it clear in his speech that he
Finds it a sheer indignity
That humans think the feline race
To be fierce and ferocious: "Nay,
Au contraire! Beauteous, strong are we…
Powerful-bodied, fair of face!"
A leopard, nodding, says his say:
"We can't deny, try though we might,
That, in the bush, our appetite
Is, to be sure… Well, rather lusty!"
And, as he carries on, so must he
Add: "What's more, when we hack to bits
A flock, stalking its tracks… No, it's
Not a mere gift to ravenous hounds!…"
Squeals a wry lynx: "Egad and zounds!
Why all the blather? Useless talk!
Rather, just own that it's our stock-
In-trade—proud creatures that we are!—
To scorn the hunter!… *Au revoir!*…

Lui réplique le Président.
Patte levée, dites-moi qui
Veut finir descente de lit ? »
Pas un fauve ne répondit !
Dès lors, le tigre proposa
En lieu et place du repas,
De faire jeûne, ce jour-là.

La prudence, royale qualité,
N'alimente pas la férocité.

120

Paw in the air, the President
Replies: "Pshaw! That's all well and good.
But tell me. If each of you could
Live out your days in life full-spent,
Who among you would choose to be
A bedside rug?… Paws up… Let's see…"
Not one paw rose. "No… I agree.
With all those 'no's I think we ought
Forget our banquet… Just a thought…"

Prudence, that royal trait, counts more
Than what our hunger murders for.

21

LE RAT ET LA CHIENNE

Un rat de cave de château
Paradait et prenait de haut
Des rats de grange et de rivière.
C'était un rat très ordinaire
Qui compensait sa petitesse
En se disant de la noblesse.
Devant la chienne de la meute,
Meneuse de la chasse à courre,
Il multipliait les mamours,
Les ronds de pattes, les ébats.
Importunée par ce pathos,
Elle requit un thérapeute,
Raton laveur de son état.
Ce gourou pratiquait l'hypnose
Si mal que son patient sombra
Et jamais ne se réveilla.
Le rat n'eut pas droit aux égards
Ni aux hommages de tribune
Mais à l'image de Mozart,
Il connut la fosse commune.

THE RAT AND THE BITCH

A haughty chateau-dwelling rat,
Proud of wine-cellar habitat,
Looked down with utter contumely
On barn-and-river rat. For he,
Small though he was, made up for that
With pretense of nobility…
Victim of love's passionate itch,
He lusted for a certain bitch—
The hound that led the hunting-pack—
Pawing her flesh, in front, in back,
With amorous revelry frenetic.
The bitch, distressed by this pathetic
Show of affection, thought that she
Ought appeal to psychiatry,
And sought out a practitioner—
A raccoon "guru," as it were—
Who, with hypnosis, put to sleep
The rat… Alackaday! Too deep
The trance! He never woke… Monsieur,
Like a Mozart of latter-day,
In pauper's grave un-honored lay…

L' ELEPHANTEAU, LE LIONCEAU ET LA GAZELLE

Parler de soi sans modestie
Ne grandit pas qui s'y résout,
Ce qu'ignore la confrérie
Des m'as-tu-vu, des mêle-tout.

« Mes parents sont tous des géants
Et mes ancêtres des mammouths
Que par le monde et de tout temps,
Peureux, prudent, l'humain redoute,
Barrit un des éléphanteaux
Aux résidents de la Réserve.
— Fils de géants que tu m'énerves !
Rugit alors un lionceau.
Sache et retiens que je te vaux !
Mon père est roi donc je suis prince.
Informe-toi si tu en doutes. »
Passe par là une gazelle.
« Qui domine ici, vous évince ?
Pas ma famille ! s'écrie-t-elle.
Chez nous, depuis la nuit des temps,
Aucun roi, pas un seul géant
Mais nous avons de grands yeux doux,
Des pattes fines et l'élégance
Des plus grands danseurs andalous.
Cela vaut bien, tout compte fait,
Votre trompe, vos deux défenses
Et l'aura d'un roi sans palais. »
Sur ce, la très jeune gazelle,
Légère et les cornes au vent,

THE ELEPHANT CALF, THE LION CUB, AND THE GAZELLE

Braggart poseurs, may well surmise:
Singing self-praise immodestly
Won't raise you in a colleague's eyes.

"Nobody in my family
Is anything less than a giant."
So trumpeted, in air defiant
And boastful tone, an elephant's
Offspring to all the occupants
Of the Reserve's domain. "What's more,
My every distant ancestor—
Terror of Man!" so he observes,
"Who wisely did his best to stay
Far as he could, out of his way—
Was the feared mammoth!…" Whence, a young
Lion cub, growing irked, unstrung,
Bellows: "You're getting on my nerves,
Giant's son! I'm a giant cat!
My father is a king, and that
Makes me a prince! And, if you doubt it,
You can just go find out about it!…"
Thereat, listening, a gazelle—
Graceful and lithe-limbed *demoiselle*—
Asks: "Who's in charge? Whose word is law?
Not me, I'm sure!… Ancestors? Pshaw!
No giants in my family tree,
No kings! But gently deft of paw
And soft of eye, I venture we
Have the elegant dignity

Rebondit entre terre et ciel
Laissant le prince et le géant
Pareillement muets, penauds
En un silence de tombeau.

Of Andalusian dancers! Surely
That is worth more, you must confess,
Than trunk, tusks, or some palace-less
King's aura!" Thereupon, demurely,
Horns to the wind, she leaps, bounds high,
Prances over their heads, 'twixt sky
And earth... The pair, with gaping jaw—
Transfixed—gaze mute, in mortal awe...

LE JURY ET LES FINALISTES

Qui s'exhibe sur un écran
Et, par jeu, sous-loue son image
Partage avec les concurrents
Les compliments et les mirages.

C'est le grand soir de la finale
Du nouveau jeu télévisé
Ouvert à la gent animale
Et en direct de la forêt.
Le public venu de partout,
Impatient, applaudit debout
Le jury et les finalistes.
A la table des jurés sont
Deux albatros et un vison
Ci-devant réputés artistes.
Face à eux s'amène, en premier,
Un sanglier haltérophile
Qui lève des cochons de lait.
Suivent sur scène peu après,
Deux varans et un crocodile
Chanteurs de blues et de reggae.
Un marabout enfin survient.
Il se dit mage et magicien.
D'un seul coup et avec succès,
Il hypnotise les jurés.
Le podium bout, la foule bruit.
Chacun soutient son favori.
Les trois chanteurs que rien n'affole
Braillent alors un rock-and-roll.
Un à un, les jurés s'éveillent

THE JUDGES AND THE FINALISTS

Ever is competition seen
Either to flatter or to flout
Those who pose on the TV screen
And blithely rent their image out.

Live from the forest! It's the night
Of the TV show's grand finale—
The talent show where shine the bright
Animal stars… No shilly-shally
Now, no more waiting, no delay,
No more suspense, deliberation…
Tonight the judges have their say.
The audience—tense!—from everywhere,
Rise up in a standing ovation,
To laud, applaud, and cheer for their
Favorite… On the platform sit
The judges, set to vote… To wit,
Two albatross, one mink: three beasts,
Themselves once much-admired artistes…
First, a weight-lifting boar, with two
Weights—suckling pigs—poised dumbbell-wise…
Second, arrive before their eyes,
Crocodile and two lizards, who—
Water-bred trio—specialize
In blues and reggae… Finally,
Comes the contestant last in line—
Stork, hypnotist-magician… He
Puts our three judges in a trance.
The crowd goes wild as all opine,
With unrestrained exuberance,

Et encore en demi-sommeil
Optent tous trois, comme en écho,
Pour un classement *ex æquo.*
Ce qui a plu, *a priori,*
Aux outsiders, aux favoris,
Les cochons de lait y compris.

In favor of this one and that,
While, un-refrained, the crooners three
Blare out a rock monstrosity,
Waiting for the result… Whereat,
The judges, one by one, awake—
Almost—and, half-asleep, they make
A quick decision: "It's a tie!"
Contestants—best, worst—pleased thereby,
Share in their rare TV success.
(The suckling pigs, no less, I guess…)

LA BREBIS ET LE VIEUX BÉLIER

Pourquoi se boucher les oreilles
Lorsque des anciens vous conseillent ?
C'est ce que se dit aujourd'hui,
Mais un peu tard, une brebis.

« Vivez les yeux levés,
Le danger vient du ciel.
Il n'y a pas là-haut
Que des vols d'hirondelle,
Des étoiles qui dansent,
Répète un vieux bélier
Aux agneaux du troupeau
Avant la transhumance. »
Une des brebis bêle :
« A quoi bon tant de zèle !
La montagne, dit-on,
N'est pas une prison.
On peut brouter à l'aise,
En toute liberté,
Courir, dormir en paix.
Où donc est le danger
En dehors des falaises ? »
Le troupeau rassuré
Où nul ne se méfie
Quitte la bergerie
Avec chiens et berger,
Monte vers les alpages,
Oublie le vieux bélier

THE EWE AND THE OLD RAM

"Why turn a deaf, disdainful ear
When elder offers good advice?"
So asked a ewe today… I fear
She asked too late. Lamb paid the price.

"Listen to me! Live with your eyes
Raised to the heavens if you would spare
Yourselves much grief. For that is where
Great danger lies! Would you be wise?
Beware! On high, all is much more
Than swallows' flight. All is not merely
Stars flickering in the skies!…" Before
The flock, about to make its yearly
Upland return, those, an old ram's
Sage words, would warn the callow lambs.
"Why such concern?" bleats a young ewe.
"The mountain is no prison! We
Are free to do what we would do,
Grazing in perfect liberty,
Leaping, sleeping our peaceful sleep…
No danger but the cliffs for us…"
Listening as she reasons thus,
Reassured by her calm, our sheep
Quit their fold, seek the pasture-grounds
Above—a-capriole, a-leap—
And quite forgetting what the old
Ram, in his wisdom, had foretold…
With shepherd-lad and faithful hounds,

Aux paroles trop sages.
Tout se passe, au sommet,
D'abord on ne peut mieux.
Chacun va où il veut
Jusqu'au jour où gracieux,
Impérial et géant,
Un aigle brusquement
En plein ciel apparaît.
Et dans les airs, altier,
Il se fait menaçant,
S'abat, serres au vent,
Et prend au dépourvu
Un des doux agnelets
Que nul n'a plus revu.

They reach the top. All goes as planned,
Until, soaring the summit-land,
One day, in graceful sweep, an eagle
Looms up—his mighty wings outspanned
In proud, majestic haughtiness
Coursing the sky, baring his regal
Talons, claws clenched and conscience-less—
Swooped… Scooped a lamblet… Skyward rose,
And whisked him off…

Whereto?… Nobody knows.

LES SOURIS ET LE MAGICIEN

Les souris grises d'une grange
Jalousaient une souris blanche
Qui vivait chez un magicien
Parmi lapins et tourterelles.
« Pour qui la blanche se prend-elle ?
Elle parade, nous dérange,
Lança une jeune jalouse
A haute voix, avec dédain.
Son magicien la sort en douce
D'un chapeau et se croit malin.
Ce n'est qu'un artiste de rue
Qui fait ses tours et vous salue
Juste avant d'assumer la quête. »
Mise au parfum, la souris blanche
Sans se fâcher clame et répète
En se postant devant la grange :
« Réservez-moi votre dimanche
Et ce jour-là, je vous invite
A une prestation gratuite. »
Ce qui eut lieu comme annoncé !
Ce que les grises ignoraient,
C'est que le magicien miteux
Etait aussi cracheur de feu
Et de la plus belle manière.
           Epouvantées,
               Les invitées
En s'enfuyant, pétaradèrent
Comme des souris à moteur.
Un rat assure que plusieurs

THE MICE AND THE MAGICIAN

Barn-bred gray mice, of base condition,
Envied a white mouse, jealously,
Who lived with a certain magician;
Rabbits and doves, her company.
"Who does that white mouse think she is?"
A scornful young gray blurted. "She
Struts by in her pomposity,
While the magician, doffing his
Top hat, with solemn sorcery,
Reaches in and discovers her!
Only a sidewalk-conjurer
Is he, whose prestidigitation
Is mere excuse for a donation!"
Informed, the white mouse, graciously—
Standing out, near their barn—extends
The following invitation: "Friends,
This Sunday, be my guests. Come see
A free performance!…" Sunday came,
And mice, watching the magic act,
Discover a disturbing fact:
Our moth-eaten magician's fame
Rests on the talents—frightful, very!—
Of fire-eater extraordinary:
Swallower, he, of torch and flame!
As he spits fire, the rodent guests—
      Fear in their breasts,
      Frantic their cackle—
Flee, like a jet, their damned debacle…
A rat, who watched their frantic flight,

Après une telle frayeur
Sont devenues blanches de peur
Prouvant ainsi, avec raison,
Que le dédain fait le dindon.

Swore that fear turned some of them white…
Deduce?… Disdain, played fast and loose?
Disdainer gets to play the goose! *

---

* Purists will argue that *dindon* means turkey. To which the translator will
reply that said fowl is used familiarly in French for a ninny, nincompoop,
etc., much as—across the language divide, maintaining the barnyard
metaphor—a "silly goose" is used in English.

LE GRAND RÊVE DE L'ORNITHORYNQUE

Chaque matin, tôt,
Au café du zoo,
Un ornithorynque
Boit un expresso,
Croque sur le zinc
Un ou deux œufs durs
Puis de cage en cage,
Il peint sur les murs
De grands paysages
Où il se dessine
Au milieu, en flou.
Cet ornithorynque
Qu'un pinceau requinque
Passe pour un sage,
Pas pour un gourou.
Mais nul ne devine
Son rêve absolu :
Faire des croisières
Autour de la Terre
Et, le temps venu,
Terminer sa vie
En son Australie.

Tout songe secret
Freine les regrets.

THE PLATYPUS'S SECRET DREAMS

At daybreak, in the Zoo
Café, the platypus—
Mammal oviparous—
Drinks his espresso, cracks
A hard-boiled egg or two,
After which, he makes tracks
From cage to cage… And he
Paints with deft artistry,
In each, a landscape, where,
Sporting a thoughtful air,
Our ornithorhyncus,
With brushstrokes decorous,
Stands posing, dreamingly,
In every scene… And thus,
In manner vague, he might,
Himself, be seen to be
A sage among the sages—
Thinker deep!—though not quite
A guru for the ages!
But no one hits upon
The dreams driving him on:
To cruise the Seven Seas
To the Antipodes,
And, in the end, once more—
Before his obsequies—
Tread his Australian shore…

Regrets are trumped, it seems,
Only by secret dreams.

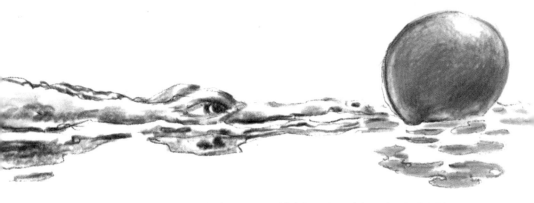

LES ALLIGATORS ET LA BOUEE

Deux alligators des bayous
Se disputaient une bouée,
Une bouée en caoutchouc
Arrivée là on ne sait d'où.
Pattes rivées sur leur trophée,
Ils se défiaient, ils battaient l'eau
Sans jamais se montrer brutaux.
A la vue de cette empoignade,
Bien des curieux se rassemblèrent,
Bien des paris furent ouverts
Annoncés à la cantonade.
Ce qui plut aux deux combattants
Lesquels, par jeu, faisaient semblant,
Semblant de se livrer bataille
Et de se tanner les écailles.
Quand la bouée se dégonfla
Sans qu'un vainqueur ne fût connu,
Les parieurs pris au dépourvu
Improvisèrent un débat.
Chacun soutint son favori.
Mais bientôt, à force de cris,
De rivalités animales,
La bagarre fut générale.
      Ce voyant,
       Sur-le-champ,
Les alligators des bayous
Interloqués, mirent les bouts.

THE ALLIGATORS AND THE BUOY

Two alligators, bayou-bred,
Were bickering, devil-may-care,
Over a rubber buoy. Each said:
"It's mine!" though neither knew just where
It came from, or whose find it was.
Each clinging with tenacious claws,
They splashed about good-naturedly,
In manner mock-pugnacious, while
Onlookers gathered round to see
Which of the pair would reconcile
This boisterous blather. Many a bet
Was taken, as to which would get
The upper-claw! Which pleased our two
Disputants, who—fierce, fiery-eyed—
Feigned the intent, with much to-do,
To tan the other's scaly hide,
Hell-bent on alligatorcide!…
When the buoy gasped its last, deflated
Without a winner consecrated,
The animal onlookers, all—
Incensed!—with blustering bray and brawl,
Debated who had lost and won.
Soon, recommenced their rivalries
As their time-honored enmities
Burst in a wild hullabaloo!
        At that—undone,
        Aghast—the two

Quant aux parieurs restés debout,
Il leur resta le caoutchouc.

Qui fait fi de la tolérance
Nourrit souvent la violence.

Erstwhile combatants promptly seize
The chance to leave. And so they do…
Bettors are left with what had been
The rubber buoy, worn out, done in…

When some pretend to disagree
        Violently,
Often real violence will break out,
        Round and about.

LE RENARD ET LE ROBOT

Affamé, de nuit, un renard
S'aventura dans un manoir.
   Il croyait y trouver
   De quoi se régaler :
Une volaille bien nourrie
Courant, de jour, dans la prairie,
Une poule, un paon, un canard,
Une pintade ou un dindon,
Une caille, un coq, un pigeon.
« Lorsque la panse crie famine,
Glapit le goupil meurt-de-faim,
A quoi bon faire grise mine,
Oser une moue de dédain ! »
Il erra dans le bâtiment
De pièce en pièce, sans succès.
Rien à se mettre sous la dent,
     Pas même un rat
     Ou un ramier.
Comme il allait sortir de là,
Il trouva un laboratoire,
Un de ces lieux ultrasecrets
Où des cobayes y sont stockés.
Le canidé reprit espoir,
Poussa la porte, et dans le noir,
Il vit s'éclairer, tout de go,
Un grand robot aux yeux fluo.
L'affamé en fut si surpris
Qu'il en perdit tout appétit
Et jura de se limiter
Aux poulaillers de la vallée.

THE FOX AND THE ROBOT

A famished fox, abroad one night,
Happening on a manor-house,
   Snuck his way in. He might,
   Thought he, find duck, quail, grouse,
Cock, peacock, turkey—even pigeon!
Something to fill his gaping gut:
One of those fine, fat fowls a-strut
By day… Be it the merest smidgeon!
"When empty belly howls its pain,"
Cried the poor wretch, "what good is it
To cast a prideful eye's disdain
On even the least little bit?"
And so, he will go wandering through
Room after room… Below, above…
       But nothing! No!
       No rat, no dove,
To sink his eager teeth into…
Nothing to eat… Defeat! And so,
Time to leave… But—so goes the story—
He finds there a laboratory.
One of those super-secret places
Teeming with guinea pigs galore!
Hopeful, pushing ajar the door,
Suddenly, in the dark, he faces
A robot monster, looming there,
Flashing its fluorescent eyes!…
Horror!… Dread!… And the Canine race's
Scion gazes in stark surprise…
Dead now that appetite! No more
His hunger wracks him!… And he swore
Henceforth the henhouse will be where
He'll go to fill his bill of fare!

L'EPHEMERE ET
L'ARAIGNEE D'EAU

Un beau matin, sur l'onde claire
D'un des étangs des Trois Herbières
  Une araignée d'eau
  Voit un éphémère
  Jaillir des roseaux.
Il paraît fragile et si frêle
Que l'araignée sitôt le hèle,
Se dit prête à le protéger
Des mille et un pièges cachés
Que les bords de l'étang recèlent.
Le protégé s'avoue flatté
Par une pareille attention.
Lors, tous deux se lient d'amitié.
L'araignée d'eau se fait bergère.
Elle chouchoute l'éphémère,
L'éloigne des bancs de poissons,
Le divertit et le conseille.
La nuit venue, elle le veille.

THE MAYFLY AND THE
WATER-SPIDER

One morning, in the sparkling air
Over the waves of Trois Herbières, *
    Kind Water-Spider sees
    Mayfly a-flit. And he's
So frail, so fragile flying there
Among the grass and reeds, that she's
Moved to try to protect him from
The myriad traps—the thousand-some
Hidden hazards, and even more—
That lurk about the marshy shore,
Lying in wait. And Mayfly, he,
Most flattered, will forthwith become
Fast friends with her. And Spider, she,
Shepherds the helpless creature here
And there, and coddles the poor dear
With wise good cheer, steering him past
The schools of fish… And when, at last,
Day dips to night, she staunchly stands

Mais quand sur l'eau, cahin-caha,
Se leva une aube nouvelle,
L'éphémère ne daigna pas
S'éveiller ni bouger les ailes.
Ce voyant, l'araignée l'évente
Et après une vaine attente,
Alerte un papillon de nuit
Lequel vient se poser sans bruit
Près de l'éphémère immobile.
« Il a vécu, soupire-t-il.
Le temps de vie est parfois court.
Le mien un mois, le sien un jour.
Consolez-vous ! Une amitié
Fait fi de tout calendrier,
Des ans, des mois, des jours, des heures.
C'est écrit dans le cœur des fleurs. »

On guard! But when, next day, the sands
Brighten beneath the morn's new light,
What's this she sees? The sleeping mite
Fails to awake, or even make
The slightest flutter! Spider, quite
Distraught, dismayed, proceeds to shake
Her protégé, and fan his brow…
No use! Utterly still, somehow…
"What now?" she asks, in her distress,
A sundown butterfly, poised near
The mite, lying yet motionless.
Sighing, he says: "His time, I fear,
Is done. Quickly life flies away—
Mine in a month, his in a day!
But be consoled. Friendship cares not
A jot for calendars' swift lot.
It defies years, months, days, and hours—
But dwells deep in the hearts of flowers!"

---

*   Scarcely a speck on the landscape, Trois Herbières is a trio of small
    ponds in the Belgian town of Les Herbières, in the province of
    Hainaut, not far from the author's home in Jurbise.

LES CASTORS ET LA CRISE

Une famille de castors
Econome comme il se doit
Est si inquiète sur son sort
Qu'elle vit sans cesse aux abois.
« En ces temps de crise mondiale,
Déclare le chef de famille,
Nous changeons notre train de vie
Et nous nous serrons la ceinture.
Nous vivotons tant bien que mal.
On est fourmis chez les cigales. »
Leurs voisins ont l'oreille dure.
« Ce castor n'a pas de ceinture
Il ne voyage pas en train,
Souffle une loutre, l'air malin.
— Nos fourmis, dit un rat musqué,
N'ont jamais vu, je le signale,
L'ombre d'une ombre de cigale. »
Se sachant incompris, moqués,
Les castors sont demeurés dignes.
Et sur ce, ont déménagé
Du côté du lac où des cygnes,
Danseurs et maîtres de ballet,
Sont, paraît-il, bien plus à l'aise
Avec notre langue française.

THE BEAVERS AND THE CRISIS

A thrifty beaver family
Does all it can to make ends meet.
Worried by the economy
And world's worsening balance-sheet,
The clan elder declares: "Though we
Keep trucking on our way as best
We can, I fear we're so hard-pressed
That, unless the conditions brighten,
It's clear we're going to have to tighten
Our belts! No more the sycophants,
The grasshopper among the ants!" *
Neighbors who hear him are not very
Subtle of ear or literary!
"That beaver," says an otter—clever!—
"Never travels by truck, and never
Wore a belt to hold up his pants!"
A muskrat, too, leering askance,
Affirms to his brother eavesdroppers:
"What's more, I doubt he ever saw
The merest shadow of grasshoppers!"
Amid many a sneered guffaw,
Beavers retain their calm *sang-froid,*
And, without fuss or tra-la-la,
Move to another apt location:
A lake where swans—a-glide, a-dance—
Treat language with more elegance,
And even much sophistication;
Where—idiom-wise—less dense for sure,
They know well their French literature…

---

* The obvious reference is to Aesop's fable about the thrifty ant and the
  spendthrift grasshopper, made famous by Jean de La Fontaine (who,
  for whatever reason, transforms the latter into a cicada with no harm
  to the moral).

LA GRENOUILLE ET LE HERON

Une grenouille de la mare
S'est levée avec le cafard.
Elle saute sans crier gare
Sur une fleur de nénuphar.
Et elle harangue de là-haut,
Les canards et les poules d'eau :
« Je suis grenouille et non crapaud.
Qu'on se le dise, par monts et vaux ! »
A portée de bec, un héron
Est à l'affût sur une patte.
De convoitise, avec raison,
Ses yeux s'allument et se dilatent.
« Vrai ! criaille-t-il. Je l'atteste :
Peau de crapaud est sans saveur.
Et je prétends que par ailleurs,
Il en est tout autant du reste. »
La grenouille n'est pas idiote.
Elle pressent que le long cou
N'est pas ici pour la parlote
Mais pour lui piquer le caillou.
Et elle plonge sans retard
Sous la fleur de son nénuphar.
Quant à notre héron, pas de veine !
Le grand échassier, ce jour-là,
S'est contenté d'un cancrelat.
Il n'avait pas lu La Fontaine.

THE FROG AND THE HERON

A pond-frog woke one morning. Bad
Her mood: blues, "blahs," depressed and sad…
And, without warning, forthwith had
An urge to leap. A lily pad
Was what she leapt to… Perching there,
With her most condescending air,
Addressing the pond *prolétaires*—
Water-hens, ducks—"I pray, take care
To note my proper pedigree,"
Says she. "I am a frog, you see,
And not a toad! Let that be known!…"
Meanwhile a heron, mischief-prone,
Stalking in one-foot pose, a mere
Beak-length away from her, gives ear—
Covetous fires lighting his eyes—
And, raucously agreeing, cries:
"She speaks the truth, I guarantee it.
Toad's hide is tasteless! And likewise
The rest of toad as well. So be it!"
Frog is no fool. Good sense decrees
Our long-neck heron has no mind
To indulge in mere pleasantries,
But rather must he be inclined
To take a nibble out of her.
Fast as you please, our posturer
Dives straight under the lily pad…
As for the heron: Damn! (Amen!)
No luck!… At length the long-legs had
To make do with a cockroach! He—
You can be sure—apparently
Had never read his La Fontaine.

155

NORMAN R. SHAPIRO, honored as one of the leading contemporary translators of French, holds the B.A., M.A., and Ph.D. from Harvard University and, as Fulbright scholar, the *Diplôme de Langue et Lettres Françaises* from the Université d'Aix-Marseille. He is Professor of Romance Languages and Literatures and Distinguished Professor of Literary Translation at Wesleyan University and is currently Writing and Theater Adviser at Adams House, Harvard University. His many published volumes span the centuries, medieval to modern, and the genres: poetry, novel, and theater. Among them are *Four Farces by Georges Feydeau; The Comedy of Eros: Medieval French Guides to the Art of Love; Selected Poems from Baudelaire's 'Les Fleurs du Mal'; One Hundred and One Poems of Paul Verlaine* (recipient of the Modern Language Association's Scaglione Award); *Negritude: Black Poetry from Africa and the Caribbean;* and *Creole Echoes: The Francophone Poetry of Nineteenth-Century Louisiana.*

A specialist in French fable literature, Shapiro has also published *Fables from Old French: Aesop's Beasts and Bumpkins* and *The Fabulists French: Verse Fables of Nine Centuries.* His translations of La Fontaine are considered by many to be the definitive voicing into English of this famed French poet. His critically acclaimed volumes include *Fifty Fables of La Fontaine; Fifty More Fables of La Fontaine; Once Again, La Fontaine;* and *The Complete Fables of Jean de La Fontaine,* for which he was awarded the MLA's prestigious Lewis Galantiere Prize. His monumental collection *French Women Poets of Nine Centuries: The Distaff and the Pen* won the 2009 National Translation Award from the American Literary Translators Association, as well as two 2008 PROSE Awards from the Association of American Publishers for the Best Single-Volume Reference in the Humanities and Social Sciences and for Excellence in Reference Works.

Other titles include *La Fontaine's Bawdy: Of Libertines, Louts, and Lechers; To Speak, to Tell You? Poems by Sabine Sicaud;* and *Préversities: A Jacques Prévert Sampler.* Shapiro is a member of the Academy of American Poets, and has been named Officier de l'Ordre des Arts et des Lettres de la République Française.

OLGA K. PASTUCHIV is a children's book author, painter, and commercial illustrator of things large and small, from murals, parade floats, and theater backdrops to a postcard for the St. Nicholas Anapafsas Monastery in Greece, a cookbook, several botany and poetry collections, including Anthony Walton's *Cricket Weather* (Blackberry Press), and Glenn Shea's chapbooks *Crossing To Aranmor* and *Find A Place* (Vortex Press), and the poster for his reading at Shakespeare & Co. in Paris; and Michael J. Caduto's award-winning *Riparia's River* (Tilbury House). Pastuchiv's picture book *Minas and the Fish* (Houghton Mifflin) is about a fisherman's boy she met on Karpathos Island while working on a fishing boat there. She has taught woodcut on both grade-school and college levels, and exhibited in galleries in several states and countries. She currently lives in Maine.

TITLES FROM BLACK WIDOW PRESS

TRANSLATION SERIES

A Life of Poems, Poems of a Life by Anna de Noailles. Translated by Norman R. Shapiro. Introduction by Catherine Perry.

Approximate Man and Other Writings by Tristan Tzara. Translated and edited by Mary Ann Caws.

Art Poétique by Guillevic. Translated by Maureen Smith.

The Big Game by Benjamin Péret. Translated with an introduction by Marilyn Kallet.

Capital of Pain by Paul Eluard. Translated by Mary Ann Caws, Patricia Terry, and Nancy Kline.

Chanson Dada: Selected Poems by Tristan Tzara. Translated with an introduction and essay by Lee Harwood.

Essential Poems and Writings of Joyce Mansour: A Bilingual Anthology. Translated with an introduction by Serge Gavronsky.

Essential Poems and Prose of Jules Laforgue. Translated and edited by Patricia Terry.

Essential Poems and Writings of Robert Desnos: A Bilingual Anthology. Edited with an introduction and essay by Mary Ann Caws.

EyeSeas (Les Ziaux) by Raymond Queneau. Translated with an introduction by Daniela Hurezanu and Stephen Kessler.

Fables in a Modern Key by Pierre Coran. Edited and translated by Norman R. Shapiro. Color illustrations by Olga Pastuchiv.

Furor and Mystery & Other Writings by René Char. Edited and translated by Mary Ann Caws and Nancy Kline.

Guarding the Air: Selected Poems of Gunnar Harding. Translated and edited by Roger Greenwald.

The Inventor of Love & Other Writings by Gherasim Luca. Translated by Julian & Laura Semilian. Introduction by Andrei Codrescu. Essay by Petre Răileanu.

Jules Supervielle: Selected Prose and Poetry. Translated by Nancy Kline and Patricia Terry.

La Fontaine's Bawdy by Jean de La Fontaine. Translated with an introduction by Norman R. Shapiro.

Last Love Poems of Paul Eluard. Translated with an introduction by Marilyn Kallet.

Love, Poetry (L'amour la poésie) by Paul Eluard. Translated with an essay by Stuart Kendall.

Pierre Reverdy: Poems Early to Late. Translated by Mary Ann Caws and Patricia Terry.

Poems of André Breton: A Bilingual Anthology. Translated with essays by Jean-Pierre Cauvin and Mary Ann Caws.

Poems of A.O. Barnabooth by Valéry Larbaud. Translated by Ron Padgett and Bill Zavatsky.

Poems of Consummation by Vicente Aleixandre. Translated by Stephen Kessler.

Préversities: A Jacques Prévert Sampler. Translated and edited by Norman R. Shapiro.

The Sea and Other Poems by Guillevic. Translated by Patricia Terry. Introduction by Monique Chefdor.

To Speak, to Tell You? Poems by Sabine Sicaud. Translated by Norman R. Shapiro. Introduction and notes by Odile Ayral-Clause.

forthcoming translations

Boris Vian Invents Boris Vian: A Boris Vian Reader. Edited and translated by Julia Older.

Earthlight (Claire de Terre) by André Breton. Translated by Bill Zavatsky and Zack Rogrow. (New and revised edition.)

Reality and Desire (La realidad y el deseo): New Selected Poems of Luis Cernuda. Translated by Stephen Kessler.

The Gentle Genius of Cecil Perrin: Selected Poems (1906–1956). Edited and translated by Norman R. Shapiro.

MODERN POETRY SERIES

ABC of Translation by Willis Barnstone

An Alchemist with One Eye on Fire by Clayton Eshleman

Anticline by Clayton Eshleman

Archaic Design by Clayton Eshleman

Backscatter: New and Selected Poems by John Olson

Barzakh (Poems 2000–2012) by Pierre Joris

The Caveat Onus by Dave Brinks

City Without People: The Katrina Poems by Niyi Osundare

Concealments and Caprichos by Jerome Rothenberg

Crusader-Woman by Ruxandra Cesereanu. Translated by Adam J. Sorkin. Introduction by Andrei Codrescu.

Curdled Skulls: Poems of Bernard Bador. Translated by the author with Clayton Eshleman.

Endure: Poems by Bei Dao. Translated by Clayton Eshleman and Lucas Klein.

Exile is My Trade: A Habib Tengour Reader. Translated by Pierre Joris.

Eye of Witness: A Jerome Rothenberg Reader. Edited with commentaries by Heriberto Yepez & Jerome Rothenberg.

Fire Exit by Robert Kelly

Forgiven Submarine by Ruxandra Cesereanu and Andrei Codrescu

from stone this running by Heller Levinson

The Grindstone of Rapport: A Clayton Eshleman Reader

Larynx Galaxy by John Olson

The Love That Moves Me by Marilyn Kallet

Memory Wing by Bill Lavender

Packing Light: New and Selected Poems by Marilyn Kallet

The Present Tense of the World: Poems 2000–2009 by Amina Saïd. Translated with an introduction by Marilyn Hacker.

The Price of Experience by Clayton Eshleman

The Secret Brain: Selected Poems 1995–2012 by Dave Brinks

Signal from Draco: New and Selected Poems by Mebane Robertson

forthcoming modern poetry titles

An American Unconscious by Mebane Robertson

Clayton Eshleman: *Essential Poetry*

Disenchanted City (La Ville desenchantee) by Chantal Bizzini. Edited by Marilyn Kallet and J. Bradford Anderson. Translated by J. Bradford Anderson, Darren Jackson, and Marilyn Kallet.

Funny Way of Staying Alive by Willis Barnstone

The Hexagon by Robert Kelly

Memory by Bernadette Mayer

Penetralia by Clayton Eshleman

Soraya (Sonnets) by Anis Shivani

LITERARY THEORY / BIOGRAPHY SERIES

Clayton Eshleman: The Whole Art by Stuart Kendall

Revolution of the Mind: The Life of André Breton by Mark Polizzotti

forthcoming

Barbaric Vast & Wild: A Gathering of Outside and Subterranean Poetry (*Poems for the Millennium*, v. 5) Eds: Jerome Rothenberg and John Bloomberg

WWW.BLACKWIDOWPRESS.COM